As For Me and My OUT House,
We Will Serve the Lord…

AS FOR ME AND MY OUT HOUSE,
WE WILL SERVE THE LORD...

JOHN A. BAKER

Xulon Press
2301 Lucien Way #415
Maitland, FL 32751
407.339.4217
www.xulonpress.com

© 2021 by John A. Baker

All rights reserved solely by the author. The author guarantees all contents are original and do not infringe upon the legal rights of any other person or work. No part of this book may be reproduced in any form without the permission of the author. The views expressed in this book are not necessarily those of the publisher.

Unless otherwise indicated, Scripture quotations taken from the Holy Bible, New International Version (NIV). Copyright © 1973, 1978, 1984, 2011 by Biblica, Inc.™. Used by permission. All rights reserved.

ISBN-13: 978-1-6628-2332-9
Ebook ISBN-13: 978-1-6628-2333-6

About the Book

What can happen when you run away from God's calling? Remember what happened to the biblical character Jonah, who refused to go to Nineveh. This book takes the reader on an intriguing and sometimes hysterical ministerial journey to learn the answer to this question. Filled with miracles and drama, intermingled with a host of calamities, the optimism and humor of the characters will have you applauding them. Defrauded the full value of their new home, see how God developed their faith and patience. Laugh and cry when you learn their reaction, at being sold a home that never had a septic tank, even when prior to purchase they paid for an inspection. Gasp with horror at looking down the gun barrel of an enraged woman, the near drowning of a baptismal candidate, or having to make a split-second decision to avoid driving off a cliff. This book will give you a fresh perspective and understanding of God like never before!

Table of Contents

About the Book vii
Forward. xi
The Invisible Ambassador. 1
The Alternating Miracle 9
Appalachia or Bus(t). 15
The Freshly Baked Deception. 21
Not Every House is a Home. 30
For Such a Call as This 36
The "Doggone" Tarp. 47
Lessons from Tall Tales. 52
God, Family, and Hand Sanitizer 57
"Deerly" Departed 61
The Phoenix Miracle 64
God of the Flies 70
It Lit the Evening Sky 74
When God Calls, Please Answer 80
The Appalachian Rock Salt Miracle. 85
The Appointed Anointed Detour. 89
My Gifts Were All the Buzz 96
Fire on the Mountain. 100
Slip Sliding Away. 106
The Ultimate Christmas Gift 119
The Designated Honor. 123
"He's Gonna Drown Grandma!" 132
Epilogue. 137
About the Author. 145

FORWARD

Some years ago, I wanted my daughter to have a gift that would give us both peace of mind. I purchased a name brand global positioning system (GPS) for her new vehicle. We had just delivered the car, ordered her GPS for the return trip home for the holidays and found a most unique problem when it was connected to its power source. While, it did have a set of maps electronically installed as we expected, the only map in its memory was for the island of Guam. Her problem was twofold, the GPS couldn't lead her anywhere she wanted to go in Nebraska, and if she could get to Guam, it wouldn't be by car.

Throughout my formative years, my life has been a lot like her GPS. I believed I knew where I was going; yet, I was foolishly following all the wrong maps. It was only after studying the true map (my Bible), that I learned I had been running around in circles completely lost. How many times do we place our trust in people, careers, and things only to realize all too soon, that they can fail us? This journey I take you on, is a journey of my own choosing. I knew God had a purpose for me, long ago. I had made a promise to Him as a child that one day I would become a minister. Foolishly as I got older, I thwarted Him at every turn.

As For Me and My Out House,

Here's how despite a multitude of bumps and bruises, God picked me up, dusted me off, and in the process of living life, He recalibrated my journey back to Him. I share with you some of the tears and laughter, my wife and I experienced along this journey of life.

Starting in my first week of ministry, I found myself replacing a beloved pastor. I was told the first day that I could "never fill his shoes". Being larger in girth than my predecessor, I replied, "That may be true, but he'd never fill my pants!" The ensuing laughter set the tone for my ministerial adventure.

I dedicate this book to Le Anne, my bride of thirty-seven years, as well as our three children; Chris, Toni, and Jesse. I also pay tribute to friends and mentors who I'm convinced I could never fill their shoes. Special recognition extended to my parents, Pastor and Mrs. Jack Baker, my wife Le Anne and several friends who want to remain anonymous for editing this book, men of integrity like Earl Gill, Randy Kassinger, Charles "Chuck" Hesler, Garry Sudds, John Van Zyl, Doug Hilliard, Dennis Milk, and so many others who encouraged me in some of the toughest times. Special thanks to my long-time friend Edmund Fry Jr. for the title of this book, Pastor Joe McCoy for being instrumental in getting us into the ministry, Terry and Melissa Turner for their friendship and generosity over the years, and Dr. Jack Ellis for serving as a tangible example of what it means to be an amazing father, confidante, and servant of Christ.

John A Baker
Email: pastorjohnabaker@aol.com

The Invisible Ambassador

"I will instruct you and teach you in the way you should go; I will counsel you with My loving eye on you." Psalm 32:8 (NIV)

"When it rains it pours," so the old saying goes. We had paid good money to purchase an ironclad warranty for our minivan, but for what? I knew what the local dealer's refusal to fix it meant—a long trek back to the original dealership four hours away. We had just paid over $1,400 to get the minivan working again before we moved to south Florida. Now it had started repeating the same annoying problems as it had done before. A return visit north was not what we had planned.

I was between jobs in healthcare, and after three years in that chaotic business, I was once again unemployed. I was chagrined. I didn't want to make the long journey but, I had nothing better to do. I had rarely had a vacation in recent years, so maybe a long drive would serve to clear my mind.

I remembered when we first moved to Florida; I had purchased a second car from my Dad and had driven it all the way down from Vermont. My oldest son asked me about the quality of the sound system. He was stunned when I replied, "I don't know. I never turned the radio during the whole trip." After my challenging work with many difficult and demanding individuals, I had needed the renewing elixir of silence.

My professional history was spotty. I had already flirted with five careers: radio broadcasting, social work, food service, hospital chaplaincy, and healthcare management. I used to joke that I was God's "dust bunny" in the vacuum of life, as I was frequently pulled into one chaotic mess after another. Four times in the past decade, I had rebuffed entreaties to enter the ministry. Being the son of minister, I was all too familiar with that life: long hours, low paychecks, and church-goer's short attention spans. Now, I was convinced that God was prodding me to change my mind.

As I began my trek north, I felt irritable. Who relishes spending money they can't afford on a four-hour trip to the past? It was my sad predicament. With three school-age children, we needed this vehicle desperately. As I drove, my mind replayed the career choices I had made over the past years.

Most recently, I had been summarily fired by the president of a company for an incident that happened two years prior to being hired. It's not often you arrive at work and are met by major-market television news trucks, and pushy reporters rushing at you from all directions. The reporters were demanding that I make a statement on the incident of two years ago! The bad public image that the frenzy created as they "camped" outside my facility for three days needed a quick fix. Unexpectedly, I became the fix and was abruptly fired.

I was used to balancing out days filled with a multitude of emotions, (stressful jobs do that for you). Now, as I came closer to my destination in northern Florida, my serenity surrendered to irritation. Entering the cavernous building, I was reminded that all car dealerships seem to smell alike–a mix of floor wax and new carpeting. I approached the service area and asked to speak to the manager. I knew I would have to talk to the "head honcho," or I would have to repeat my story endlessly. After conferring with the manager, he apprised me that the repairs could take as long as four days to complete–the parts had to be ordered. My prevailing thought was: four days, you've got to be kidding me! Where are they being shipped from, Singapore?

No vehicle had ever robbed me of my joy more than this "fertilizer wagon" had done. The dealership was nice enough to lend me a cheap rental car. Notice I didn't say a rental car cheap, but rather a cheap rental car. I wasn't a high-rolling customer. The vehicle looked like it had been made by Fisher Price. As I squeezed into the miniscule car's front seat, I told myself that at least I wouldn't need a box of Kleenex. My knees pressed hard against my nose would keep it from running. My irritation level was now peaking. Coupled with hunger, I desperately needed a diversion.

Resigned to a long week, I thought I'd make the best of a bad situation by revisiting a popular eatery across town. It was a favorite all-you-can-eat lunch buffet. I had been missing the old place. My mouth watered in anticipation as I cruised into the restaurant's parking lot. It was early, so I knew I could get a table more quickly than normal.

As I entered the establishment, the delectable aroma of their food reminded me of the last time I had visited. This wasn't my "first rodeo" when it came to this buffet. I positioned myself in front of the "Waitress Will Seat You" sign by the door. I was starving!!! As I patiently bided my time, I thought the waitresses were a bit rude. I could see two of them standing and talking, yet they seemed oblivious to my presence. I grew impatient as neither made a move to approach me. Several minutes passed with still no acknowledgment that I needed seating.

Moments later, the door behind me with its chime attached, announced the entrance of new guests. A middle-aged couple stood behind me waiting to be seated. On cue, one of the waitresses brushed past me, escorted them to a seat, and took their drink order. Quickly after seating them down, she picked up the conversation with her colleague – but kept ignoring me. Thinking she had just overlooked me, I walked around the sign and coughed out loud, trying to gain their attention. Despite making noise, I received no response from the waitress! The door chime dinged for the second time. As before, the waitress whizzed past me to escort the newest couple to their seats and take their drink order.

By this time, my irritation had evolved into anger. I could see the steaming tables of Mexican delicacies just feet away, yet I still hadn't been seated. Despite my attempts to be noticed, no effort had been made by the waitresses to acknowledge my presence. I became emboldened. I walked up and stood next to the cash register not seven feet away from them. I expected at least one of them to finally notice me standing close by, but they were oblivious.

It was on my third attempt to be seated when the door chime went off again, and the waitress rushed past me to seat the newest couple. I was incensed! How could I have been missed these many times? I'm a three-hundred-pound guy! At the third rebuff, I turned on my heels and stormed out muttering, "If that's the way they treat customers, I'll go somewhere else, where my business will be appreciated."

Steaming with indignation, I got into my cramped loaner car and drove along the main thoroughfare looking for an alternative restaurant. I got angrier by the minute as I thought about being summarily ignored. The nerve of them! As my eyes sought a suitable alternative, I caught sight of a large Pizza Hut sign.

A neon sign was flashing, "lunch buffet." I knew I wouldn't be overlooked at this establishment because I'd be serving myself.

I was thoroughly famished as I made my way into the semi-crowded restaurant. I had eaten there in the past, and usually at this time of day, the place would be packed. Regardless, I was encouraged that my waitress wasn't blinded to my presence, and I was quickly seated.

I smiled as I made my way from my table to the buffet deck that was loaded with salad and fresh-baked pizza. Balancing my two brimming plates, I carefully walked back to my table. As I prepared to offer a blessing over my food, I couldn't help but notice three women seated in the corner of the room. I thought it was odd that the four of us were the only ones in the second half of the two-room restaurant. Everyone else preferred being crammed into the other side near the food. Oh well, to each their own I thought as I began to eat. I was unaware that what would transpire in a few moments would be life altering for me. For you see, in this section of the restaurant, God had preset the seating arrangements.

I took note of the three attractive women, in their late twenty's, fifteen feet away as they sat at their table. I listened to their banter. Two of the women were animated while the third woman was not. She sat with her head down throughout their conversation and uttered not one word. The exchange between the friends was loud enough to overhear and their words were venomous. They were peeved, and it soon became clear it was a diatribe against men. I couldn't help but catch snippets of their conversation; men were all cads and lower than dirt. One comment was so over-the-top I couldn't help but snicker about the absurdity of their claims.

Out of the corner of her eye, one of the participants saw me chuckle and quickly drew me into the conversation by shouting across the room. "You!" she shouted boldly.

"Me?" I replied.

"Yes you! Are you married?" Before I could respond she blurted out, "You look married."

I laughed and wondered to myself, how does one look married? Going along with the indictment of "looking married," I responded, "Yes, I am married."

She continued, "Have you ever been unfaithful to your wife?" I wasn't expecting this line of questioning, especially while being yelled at from across a room.

I answered "No." It was then that the second woman jumped into the conversation with a bombshell of her own.

"What would you say about a man who not once, but three times had affairs on his wife, and has lost his career over it? Should she divorce him?"

Embarrassed by her friend's loud banter, the silent young woman in the middle cast her eyes further downward toward the floor and blushed. My first thoughts were for this this woman whose beauty and features were flawless. How could any man cheat on such a lovely person?

As I opened my mouth to respond to their questions, my response even caught me off guard. I hadn't expected this interaction today, but someone had–God. Looking directly at the brokenhearted woman I shared, "I cannot tell you what to do. I have seen marriages work through unfaithfulness, and I have seen them fall apart. The fact that your husband has been unfaithful not once, but three times at the expense of ruining his career, tells me this is not *your* fault. Don't let any member of his family, or your family, place the blame on you.

"While I personally can't give you an answer as to what you should do, I do know someone who can. I urge you to take your Bible and go to a hotel for two or three days alone. Take the phone off the hook and unplug the television. Spend time just reading the Bible and talking to God. I promise you that by the third day, you will have your answer."

After conveying that counsel, she looked up at me and mouthed softly, "Thank you." As if they were leaving a church, the three got up from their table and without another word, quietly exited the restaurant and drove away. What just happened? I was astonished. Did God send me four hours from home, to a city of one million people, just to answer the call of one hurting young woman?

For the next several days I replayed this incident in my mind. After my reluctance to say yes to the ministry so many times before, I had a lot of questions for God. Why had He sent me, an unwilling participant, on this mission trip? Was our family vehicle allowed to break down just so this encounter could take place?

My next thought was even more difficult to explain. Was the reason I hadn't been seated at the Mexican restaurant because God had made me invisible to two waitresses? It was the only plausible way to explain how I had been overlooked three times. The waitresses had been blinded to my presence, because God needed me for an hour on the other side of town.

The experiences at both restaurants initiated a season of spiritual discovery that engaged me. The epiphany that God had used me for His purpose, despite the fact my relationship with Him had been on shaky ground, intrigued me.

I'd like to say that from that moment on, His plan for my life gave me full clarity as to what I was supposed to do, but it did not. He chose to wait for me a little longer. There were more lessons I had to learn before I was prepared to assume the mantle of ministry. However, it was His next miracle that would clinch it for me.

The Alternating Miracle

"I am the Lord, the God of all mankind. Is anything too hard for me?" Jeremiah 32:27 (NIV)

God has a plethora of ways to get our attention. For a man, the two most effective methods He uses are in the taking away of his wallet or his car. When He takes both, it indicates to the man that He really means business.

My wife's minivan (the devil's tool to goad me into forgetting my Christianity), had a fried electrical system. Have you ever hated something so much that it brought you to rage? For me, it was that minivan. I used to complain that her vehicle didn't need a mechanic, it needed an exorcist. It was forever developing issues that would make it inoperable. At this point, it was sidelined by that same issue–for the second time

My car, on the other hand, wasn't much better. While functional, it was in desperate need of a visit from someone like Elijah, the biblical prophet. I would give anything to see him call down fire from heaven and consume both. Mine exhibited transmission problems, as it refused to go above second gear. My gasoline powered vehicle acted as if it were an electric car: each morning I would drive our three children to school, (never topping 35 miles per hour), then must drive home quickly and reconnect it to the battery charger. The battery wouldn't hold a charge for long and there was no money to purchase a new one.

For months, I was stuck in what seemed like a game of monotony. It was the same thing every day with absolutely no change. When experiencing setback after setback, without the ability to catch your breath, the tendency is to withdraw from people. You hate telling your story of woe because recounting it only makes you sound bitter and emotional. No one wants to dwell on their misfortunes, and they surely don't want to hear unsolicited theories by friends on why you seem to be cursed.

I was at that point. I recalled that the Bible character Job had some harsh friends too. Amidst his difficulties, they thought nothing of piling on their own "helpful" counsel that made him feel even worse–if that were possible. I felt like I wanted to jump into Job's story and exclaim to him in my own exasperation, "Pass the sackcloth and ashes my friend, I'm joining you."

I had a well-meaning friend who would call me from time to time, and though I dearly appreciated her, she had the knack of saying the most ill-timed comments. My irritation grew when we conversed. She would frequently boast about a new purchase or an amazing trip that her family had just taken. It was hard to swallow the blessings of others when my own throat was constricted from hardship.

Alone in my living room after returning from dropping off the children at school, I was heartbroken. The holidays were just weeks away, and I had one hundred and fifty dollars to my name. I didn't want to disappoint them. Unbeknownst to them, we were a mere four months from being evicted–if I couldn't find a job.

While Le Anne and I had little money to give to our church, one thing we could do was to volunteer. It was midweek and, being a talented decorator, she showed me the finer points of sprucing up the church's interior. As we sat on the front pew working on Fall floral decorations, a couple of men walked into the sanctuary unannounced. They proceeded to plead for help with gas money. Just passing through town, they were in desperate need of assistance.

Without reservation, she reached for her purse. She apologized that she had only a handful of coins to offer them. Her hands filled with the change; she gave them all that she had. They thanked us and departed. Minutes later she burst into tears. From her heart she choked, "We always give generously to help everyone else; when can we expect someone to do the same for us?" What we didn't know then was that her answer would be forthcoming shortly.

To spare our oldest son Chris the stress of my chaotic healthcare career, some old family friends offered to have him stay with them so he could attend school in Florida. It was an answer to prayer. This plan would keep him in a Christian school, spare him frequent moves, and minimize his worry about our finances–or lack thereof.

It was the week before Thanksgiving, and we had been separated from our son for months. Our friends called us; they knew our circumstances and made us an offer we couldn't refuse: "We have arranged a beautiful oceanfront beach house in Siesta Key, Florida. Please come down and join us; you won't have to worry about a thing."

I laughed to myself as I hung up the phone. The worry wasn't *when* we would arrive, it was *if* we could arrive. Le Anne and I discussed the limitations of driving seven hundred miles in a car that would not shift out of second gear, but the chance of seeing our son overruled our common sense. I managed to scrape together enough money to purchase a new battery and alternator for my car, and though it wouldn't go above forty miles an hour, at least it didn't have to be plugged in twice a day.

Our remaining family of four set out early the next morning, praying all the way. Unable to maintain the required minimum freeway speed of forty miles per hour, the car limped along country backroads. Seventeen hours later, upon arrival, the transmission fluid reservoir mirrored our energy level – it was on empty. Now, in the presence of our son and close friends, the balmy temperatures and salty ocean breezes gave us a new lease on life. It was a beautiful relaxing week, but it ended all too soon.

Over breakfast our last morning, we were discussing our return trip home. Aghast that we had traveled in such a decrepit vehicle our friends came up with an idea of driving one of their parents cars home and leaving our old one behind. Their parents were elderly and were planning to sell one anyway, they said. We quickly agreed, so the following day we were driven to Ocala where the "new" one was being repaired and said, "It's yours. Send us the money only when you have it." Everyone needs compassionate and generous friends like that. They hugged us goodbye and with Chris accompanying them, they drove back home.

As we waited for our "new" car to receive its adjustments, we were giddy with anticipation for the ride home. We would be able to travel faster than a moped, and the air conditioning and radio would be operable. Our excitement lasted all of thirty minutes. We shook our heads in disbelief as the service manager told us that as the car was being driven out of the repair bay, its engine had "blown." After the service manager apologized and pronounced our misfortune, we burst out laughing. Could anything more bizarre or ridiculous happen to us?

We were grateful to be within walking distance of a hotel, so with each of us lugging a suitcase, we made our way across the street. Now, ensconced in our room, we were at a loss about what to do next. Just as we began to plan how we would return home, we received a phone call that my beloved grandmother had passed away. We were needed in Massachusetts for the funeral, 1250 miles away.

We didn't have money or a major credit card, but we did have a Sears card; it helped us to obtain a rental car. By the grace of God, that necessary trip to New England was secured. It was a bittersweet return to my roots in New England. The funeral was a fitting tribute to a beautiful Christian woman, but it was with heavy hearts that we began the journey home. I dropped off the family at our home in North Carolina before making the extended trip back to Florida to retrieve our old car. Our friends were embarrassed that their parent's car hadn't worked for us, but misfortune was my calling card. If anyone could roll with life's uncertainties, I could. After all, wasn't I still God's "dust bunny," constantly being pulled into a whirlwind of problems?

I hugged our friends and son said goodbye a second time and began the long drive back home in our ailing car. With spotty air conditioning and still not able to get out of second gear, the ride was interminable. I kept the speedometer at 35 miles per hour and once again avoided the main roads. The quietude offered me ample time to talk, no, to *voice* my displeasure with God over our present circumstances.

Angrily, I spouted back the scripture that promised His believers they could have an abundant and overflowing life, but I was unimpressed. If I had anything in my life that remotely included an overflow, it would probably only be within the realm of bathroom plumbing. Like the Peanuts character Pig Pen, I was resigned that my lot in life would always include a persistent dark cloud over my head.

Eventually, I arrived back home and the next morning I drove the kids to school. While there, I bumped into our devout pastor and struck up a conversation. As I relayed my car's problems, he told me of a place nearby that had fixed an electrical problem for him, and best of all, their prices were reasonable. With that information in hand, I made my way to the designated shop, and left my vehicle with the proprietor.

It was only a scant twenty hours later that I received a call from the shop and was told to come retrieve my car. The best part of their call was that my vehicle's performance was fully restored for under $65. I was relieved but intrigued. What could have cost so little that I could get everything resolved, including my transmission woes?

As I entered the repair shop, the first thing the mechanic said to me was, "I bet you're glad you live around here."

"Why do you say that?" I inquired.

"Because whoever replaced your alternator and battery recently didn't wire it properly. In fact, they forgot to connect the main wire fully to the alternator." I didn't have the nerve to tell him I had just returned from Florida in that same vehicle. He finished by saying, "Yes sir, you're lucky you didn't take this on a trip because that alternator wasn't even charging."

His words left me in a daze as I walked outside to get my car. I had made my way home from Florida in a car with no power source! At that moment, I came to the realization that the more you grow in your faith with God, the more you must apologize to Him. I recalled my earlier grumbling about my supposed lack of blessings. This second miracle enlightened me. If God can bring power to a powerless vehicle, then I wanted Him to do the same thing in my life.

APPALACHIA OR BUS(T)

"For I know the plans I have for you," declares the Lord, "plans to prosper you and not to harm you, plans to give you hope and a future."
Jeremiah 29:11

I wasn't a member of the Beverly Hillbillies clan, but you wouldn't have known it by what I was driving. During the last year of my healthcare career, our family had acquired a converted 1974 International school bus from a friend. Thank goodness it was no longer canary yellow as it had been painted white. A beauty queen, it was not. The exterior looked like we should be selling snow cones at construction sites. Despite its ragtag appearance, it had served me well as a temporary home during my last healthcare assignment.

I must give the bus some credit though; it was spacious. The biggest drawback was the tongues that wagged when we pulled into one of the "nicer" RV parks. The snooty late model RV drivers probably expected us to exit the bus while wearing straw hats and overalls, as we chewed on long blades of grass. My advice is, if you need to live in a converted school bus, is to install thick curtains. This came from the lesson that, more than once, I had a few unexpected moments of being caught in my underwear. No matter which campground we used, it seemed everyone was curious to know about the interior of the bus.

To my parents and siblings, our bus was a form of embarrassment. In their eyes, we were rambling around the state in a saltine-like cracker box on wheels. I didn't care what they thought. It was paid for, and at least it wasn't a tent. Granted, the exterior needed some work, as it had a steel platform welded on the back to hold the generator, but the interior was amazing. During the summer months, Chris and I transformed the interior décor of the bus by using a log cabin theme. The embossed pine log wallpaper, woodsy accents of moose and bear, and checked green curtains completed the country charm. It boasted all the comforts of home: a full bathroom, kitchen, pantry and four beds. The most popular feature, especially with friends of our children, was a fully functional satellite TV setup.

I had finally agreed to accept a new role in Appalachia as a district pastor of three small rural churches. So, in July, we headed to our new Kentucky assignment via Interstate 75. Driving our monstrosity required patience. I soon discovered how daunting it was driving up steep mountain inclines with an underperforming engine. I kept the gas pedal mashed to the floor, but a getaway vehicle it was not. As I drove slowly in the breakdown lane, cars were hurtling past me as if I were stopped. The bus almost was. My two-barrel carburetor could barely muster a robust ten miles an hour as we crested mountain after mountain. I imagined Scotty, from *Star Trek*, yelling in his Scottish brogue his famous words, "I'm giving her all she's got, Captain!"

My wife and children, driving behind in the family car, had the flashers on and the air conditioning off. I can only imagine their discomfort as they trailed behind the bus while it spewed out clouds of black exhaust. The smoke was so thick that it looked like we were spraying the roadside to keep pests under control.

As we crested the mountain peaks, the clickity-clack rattling of the gas stove burners in the kitchen gave me reason to celebrate; we were picking up speed! The trip from Florida had had its share of surprises. Like the fictional pioneer travelers in the computer game *Oregon Trail,* I hoped we would be spared dysentery, scurvy, and tribal raids in our new Appalachian wilderness home. I was unaware that I should be thanking God for shielding us from being able to know our future.

Our new pastoral assignment had brought us to an unsophisticated small rural town. Housing was hard to come by so we parked the bus behind our new church and camped out for what we thought would be a short period of time. Though it was tedious for Le Anne and me, the children found the experience delightful. In the weeks ahead the search for a new home was grueling, but it had taken a backseat to the needs of our three country churches. Following four months of searching for a home, we finally found one. And, it had a space to park the bus. Now with the promise of more room to spread out, we happily settled in after all the preliminaries were filled and the mortgage paperwork signed. The fullness of the what we purchased as opposed to what we thought we purchased, is detailed in the next chapter.

Meanwhile, the following May, like all the ministers in my conference region, we were required to attend and work an old-time camp meeting in central Tennessee. These meetings were scheduled to last two weeks including setup and take down of the tents. I thought it best to make use of our RV bus. Our own self-contained home would be a better alternative than having to share bathroom facilities with dozens of other attendees in a dormitory setting. At least we could have our privacy. Leaving the rest of the family at home to join us later, our now teenage son Chris and I embarked on an odyssey that, to this day, has bonded us for life.

The trip that would under normal circumstances take about five and a half hours to complete, turned into a thirteen-hour nightmare. As long as the old bus had no hills to climb, it could make decent speeds. Approaching even a gently sloped hill reduced our speed to a crawl. What we didn't know at the time, was that the carburetor was stuck open, and gas was pouring into the chamber faster than it could burn.

We soon realized that the manifold was turning bright red from the fiery heat as the overabundance of fuel was igniting. As the pressure in the engine increased, it would seep oil from the over-strained gasket. When the oil hit the red-hot manifold, it would combust. This meant that for hours we could only travel at speeds between fifteen to twenty miles per hour, with frequent stops to put out the recurring flames. We were fortunate that on the first twelve hours of the drive (with flashers on), we encountered no police cars. We would, no doubt, have been pulled over for driving too slowly.

It was now one a.m. and we had five hours before we needed to be at our destination. It was imperative that we arrive on time, as we were responsible for cooking the meals for the meetings. As we neared Bowling Green, Kentucky ready to enter the busy freeway, we decided to give the bus and us a much-needed rest. The engine needed to cool down. If the engine was cool, it could run for about forty minutes at speeds up to fifty miles per hour–then it would overheat. It was our hope that this little respite, and window of opportunity, would get us to our exit in Tennessee–before it would quit.

We began driving anew at 4:00 a.m., and as we closed in on the Tennessee state line, we were quickly losing power. We were once again at the forty-five-minute mark of the bus's performance window. The engine was burning red hot, and the loss of power found us crossing the state line doing just thirty-five miles per hour. As we approached our exit, that was when I noticed flashing red and blue lights behind us. A state trooper was pulling us over, no doubt for driving below the minimum speed limit.

Even though we could see our exit a mere hundred yards away, we had to pull to the side of the road to comply with the law. Figuring it could take some time for the officer to run a check on the license plate, I decided to let the engine cool down. I watched the young trooper make his way cautiously behind our bus just as I made the ill-fated choice to switch off the ignition.

I can only describe what happened next as hearing the loudest booming howitzer west of Baghdad. To someone standing close by, the shockwave that whooshed through the exhaust pipe must have sounded like a hydrogen bomb being detonated. Kabooooooom! The hillsides reverberated with thunder. In the rearview mirror, I saw the fastest running trooper in all of Tennessee history dive into his car, throw it in reverse, and peel rubber. After he was at least eight car lengths behind us, he jumped out of his vehicle. Using his open car door as a shield, he crouched behind it and bellowed into his loudspeaker, "COME OUT OF THE VEHICLE NOW!

As we exited the bus, feeling rather embarrassed, Chris fell into a fit of laughing. In my sternest voice, I whispered at him to stop. He only laughed louder. The officer was not amused. Still crouching behind his car door, he demanded, "What the (expletive) is going on?" All things considered; we probably did look a bit like we were rejects from the cast of *Deliverance*.

I hollered back to him that we were headed to some religious meetings. He quickly yelled back on his loudspeaker, "You are NOT going any further on this highway!" His emphasis was clearly on the word not! I yelled back to him that it was okay, as the exit I was now pointing too was the one we were wanting. Emphatically, he ordered us back into the bus and with authority declared, "I'll escort you off the highway NOW!" With his lights still flashing, he followed us the remaining 100 yards to our exit. Turning on a dime, he zipped by us then quickly took an immediate left-hand turn and he sped back toward the state line rest area, no doubt to change his undergarments.

My son and I laughed our relief and exhaustion away while we drove the remaining miles into town for our dawn appointment. It's not often you get away with "pranking" a police officer, even though it was unintended. Reflecting on that episode, I've often wondered as to what religion he might have thought we belonged; I was reluctant to even guess. Our experience proved one old adage true, "If you're going to do it right, go out with a bang."

The Freshly Baked Deception

"Whoever walks in integrity walks securely, but whoever takes crooked paths will be found out."
Proverbs 10:9 (NIV)

The time we lived in our bus after arriving at our new church district was now approaching five months. However difficult it was for the family; it was approaching a full year for me and I was feeling cramped. I was grateful for our home on wheels, but even Superman must have wished for a better place to change than a narrow phone booth. As eager as we were to depart the confines of the churchyard, where our bus temporarily sat, we were certain the church members would be even happier to have the eyesore off their property.

It was a bright autumn day when our real estate agent called to inform us that she had found a house we would like. Eager to finally have more room to spread out, we agreed to meet her there. The cute brick home had just come on the market today. The house we were being shown was the first one that seemed promising. Its curb appeal was attractive, but we were skeptical as we pulled into the driveway. The home was situated in a low-lying area not far from a stream.

Due to the mountainous terrain, many homes in Appalachia are often erected between notched mountain sides called coves or "hollers," (between two mountains). Still others are on such steep mountain sides that it makes you wonder how they were ever erected, looking as though they had been set into place by a helicopter. Because of water runoff, these "hollers" are often adjacent to rivers and streams. This one was.

In the past, the three important lessons we learned regarding home ownership were: always get a home inspection, read the local floodplain maps, and stay away from homes where the neighbors have cars without tires, balanced on cement blocks in their front yard. Any of these factors would potentially contribute to the amount of antacid or aspirin you would have to consume on a daily basis. This home's driveway, while not technically in a flood plain, was situated just across the street from one.

Our agent, sensing our misgivings, assured us that floodwaters had never reached the house or the neighbor's house across the road. She stressed that high water had only *approached* the neighbor's large backyard a few times. Without speaking, my wife and I locked eyes. It was a communication skill honed by years of marriage. We quickly proclaimed, "Ah…nope." My father had a philosophy about my luck: "You remind me of the guy who bought a suit jacket and two pairs of matching pants – then burned a hole in the jacket." This was not the house for us.

We told her that while the home itself had features we liked, we didn't want to take a chance on it. She pressed us to reconsider. Trying to allay our fears, she assured us that a flood had *never* come close to approaching this home in the hundred-year history of the neighborhood. We refused to be persuaded – this was the one hundred and first year! If there was even a one percent chance of calamity, we knew that if we owned that abode there could be countless ways that it might be destroyed: termites… watery mudslides… fire… a direct lightning strike… a stray meteorite. She couldn't budge us from our determined position.

Getting back into the car, she chided, "You missed a golden opportunity." Unconvinced, we walked away from her "gem," as she referred to it. Later, it would prove to play prominently in how we dealt with adversity in the days ahead. No matter what awaited us, this home would be a reminder that things could always be worse. Less than four years later, during torrential rains, this "gem" was destroyed, and swept away with others along that valley stream.

Despite the disappointment of not finding the home we needed, we were undaunted and continued to pray for God to show us the one He wanted us to have. A few weeks later my cellphone rang, and I heard the words, "I've found it!" Our agent excitedly exclaimed, "The house I've found for you was just listed today. You have to see it!" She was certain that we would love the place, and went on to describe in glowing terms, what sounded like a better find than we could have hoped for. The owners were being transferred and needed to sell their beautiful brick home. It was located on the side of a mountain, offered panoramic views of the valley, and was a spacious 2,100 square feet. It was *not* near a swollen creek.

We happily toured the house several times. On each visit, the sweet aroma of apple-cinnamon candles and fresh-baked cookies was evident. We were impressed with the homeowner's domestic skills. It would be later that we learned why she possessed such a passion for baking. On one of our visits, we asked her why they were moving. She replied that it was because of a job transfer. If we were to purchase her home, she said that the transition would be seamless, since a government agency would handle the sale and purchase details.

With our financing approved, and all the precautionary measures taken that verified the good condition of the house, we signed the final papers a week before Thanksgiving. The moving-in process was arduous, as our one-hundred-foot driveway was steep. We had to park the moving van a mile away and use a smaller truck that was able to navigate up to our entrance.

Le Anne was a marvel when it came to moving and organization. I'm convinced that if General Eisenhower could have used her skills to plan D-Day, it would have been over in a mere twenty-four hours. In that amount of time, she had unpacked and settled us into our new "dream home."

Our first official guest was the realtor who had sold us our home. She appeared at our door to present us with a housewarming gift. Her family pet accompanied her on the visit. As she entered our doorway, her aging male dog was on a mission of his own. Without hesitation, he ran to the corner of the living room, lifted his leg, and watered our Ficus tree. Our realtor was mortified, but looking back, I realized that the dog was not just committing an embarrassing act. No, he was sending us a symbolic message that we would soon discover; this plant wasn't the only thing that would be "soaked."

A few weeks later, at the end of December, we became aware of a few annoyances in the house. We noticed our first electric bill was extremely high. We began to wonder if our small town had plugged extension cords into outlets on the outside of our house and we were paying everyone's bill. Did our house have any insulation at all? The stringent requirements of our Rural Housing loan stipulated that the house had to have proper amounts of insulation under the floor joists and in the walls and attic. And why all of a sudden, were we detecting the smell of sewer gas so strongly?

I decided to find the answers to these questions, so I donned an old pair of jeans and a flannel shirt then grabbed a flashlight. On this freezing winter afternoon, I was on a mission. As I scrabbled along the crawlspace, I was convinced that with the cold weather, it was unlikely that I would make the acquaintance of any snakes. I accept my blessing as I get them, but that would be the only good news I would have that day.

Brushing away cobwebs, dirt, and dampness, I was devastated by what I discovered. As I inched my way toward the back of our house, what I discovered shocked me: virtually every floor joist at the back was either fractured or broken. While this was distressing and disheartening, it was just the beginning. Why had our home inspector not identified and listed this problem? If he had such an apparently well-deserved reputation, why did our broker and mortgage lender utilize his services? And hadn't we prayed for God to guide us to the house He wanted us to have?

In the days ahead we learned that our home inspector was known for being so unscrupulous, that he'd earned a descriptive addition to his first name. It was "Drive-By." The movie character, Forest Gump, summed up life with his mamma's philosophical words: ... "Life is like a box of chocolates. You never know what you're gonna get." For us, our home would become equal parts money pit and horror show. We'd been duped by old "Drive-By."

Despite reporting and showing proof of the fraudulent anomalies in our house purchase, our lender and broker chose to ignore us. I had identified five violations of The Fair Housing Act that should have triggered an investigation, but the mortgage purchaser refused to act or answer our pleas. Our letter to the state attorney general's office was rebuffed by a response of, "Organize protestors from your church. Arrange for them to picket the state house then maybe you can get some press exposure on your plight."

To ascertain the full extent of the fraud that had been perpetrated, we hired a reputable inspector from the county south of us. He spent the better part of a day doing a thorough investigation. His pile of written notes was extensive. Two weeks later, he presented us with a written estimate. The damages totaled more than $83,000. To say we were shocked was an understatement as we had just which purchased our home for $92,000. On the outside, it was beautiful. But it was almost as fragile as a house made of cards. If it weren't repaired soon, it was capable of collapsing.

Despite the discouraging house situation, we still had a job to do. We had three churches under our pastoral care. When the members heard about our plight, they naturally wanted to know what we intended to do. There sometimes comes a point in life when things become so beyond bearing that you can only laugh. We were at that point. There was no way, or money available to fix these kinds of problems on our own. We left everything in God's capable hands and focused on our ministerial calling.

The first major event, after learning about our structural damage, occurred six months later. We blew out an underground waterline. The previous owner had used a low-pressure line to hook up to the high-pressure county water system so the underrated water pipe couldn't handle the pressure. We were desperate for a quick repair but, of course, the pipe had burst on the 4th of July weekend. It would be impossible to hire a backhoe and plumbing company until the weekend was over, so we relied on our above-ground pool as our only source of water.

Monday morning arrived. I thumbed through the yellow pages and secured help from a local plumbing company. Being desperate, I engaged the unfamiliar group. Early next morning, three men showed up to work on the lines. Looking as if they had just come from another job, their clothes were grossly dirty and stained. I silently questioned my choice of plumbers. Nevertheless, I appreciated their enthusiasm as they got to work.

They began digging up the driveway in order to determine where the water pipe was leaking. They soon learned that the previous owner was not a good fix-it man. The inferior waterline he had used, from the house to the water meter one hundred feet down our hillside, was all going to have to be replaced. The replacement took two days to complete but, as it turned out, they had barely begun to make our needed repairs. When they turned the water back on at the foot of the hill, the waterlines under the house began to spout water like party favors that unroll when you blow into them. Now, it was *their* turn to crawl underneath our house and investigate.

They came out with samples of what they had found. The pipes were being held together with car radiator clamps, hoses, and hydraulic plastic sleeves. Nothing had been soldered in the proper way. Additionally, the plumbers were upset when they discovered that the toilets had not been vented through the roof as required by code. They had merely lopped off a five-inch notch on top of the sewer drain and let the gases self-vent into the crawlspace.

They became even more upset when they realized they had been using their acetylene torches in a space where the sewer gas had been accumulating. Summing up the situation, one of the workers emphatically stated, "We coulda blowed up this thing, with us in it!" It slowly began to dawn on us why the lady had been baking each time we came to view the house: the friendly baked-goods cinnamon candle aromas had been used to cover up the smell of sewer.

Knowing their job was going to be much more involved than they had reckoned, they summoned me to discuss the situation. Tired and muddy from their efforts, they sat down on the front lawn. I looked the head crewman directly in the eye.

"What's it like under there?"

He didn't sugarcoat his reply, unlike the previous freshly baked deceptions we had experienced. He said simply, "It's awful bad!"

"How bad is bad?" I asked.

"The worst I *ever* seed!" he drawled.

Envisioning more money slipping through my fingers, I inquired, "What do you suggest we do to repair what's wrong?"

"Well," the man paused, as if he was unsure of my response. "I know someone who 'ill burn it down fur a thousand dollars."

I burst into a hearty laugh, until I saw the look on both their no-nonsense faces. He continued, "Seriously, a thousand dollars will take care of it."

At that point, I realized they weren't kidding. "No, I better not do that. Just fix what you can." Shrugging their shoulders as if to say, "You're crazy but suit yourself," they began their ongoing task.

Later that week, I visited a policeman friend and shared with him the criminality of what the plumbers had offered. Thinking that my friend would agree with me that offering arson as a plumbing option was a completely corrupt and despicable idea, I was taken aback by his response. Incensed, he responded with "That's terrible! A thousand dollars is ridiculous! Five hundred dollars is max for burning down a problem house." As I drove home after my visit, I couldn't help but wonder if anyone would ever believe our story.

By the year's end, the fallen autumn leaves dropped by the trees on our hillside were long faded from their golden-yellow and russet-red colors. They were now a discouraging sepia tone. The dazzling fall display was over, as was our former enthusiasm for our house. In the nine years that we lived in that home, I'm certain that I was the plumbing company's most frequent customer. In fact, I had their phone number on speed dial. Would this house ever be right?

Not Every House is a Home

> "Blessed is the one who perseveres under trial because, having stood the test, that person will receive the crown of life that the Lord has promised to those who love Him." James 1:12 (NIV)

We had experienced a lot of rain lately, but Spring was like that in Appalachia. It had been four days since our twelve-year-old daughter Toni and her eight-year-old brother Jesse had been able to go outside. Now at last we had a nice day, so they went into our backyard for some sun and exercise. I decided to take a break too and was just lying down to read when I heard, "Dad! Dad come quick. There's a sinkhole in our yard and it smells terrible!"

Hearing Jesse's strange pronouncement, I jumped up and grabbed my jacket. What in the world was this new snafu? We had endured an unusually long rainy season, and now as I stared in disbelief at the deep hole in our yard, my first thought was that our old septic tank must have collapsed. I found my phone and tapped the speed dial once again to reach our friends at the plumbing company. They were not surprised to hear from us.

The following day, after a fast inspection, we received a definitive answer.

"We got good n' bad news fer ya. The good news is it ain't the septic tank."

Relieved, I responded, "Oh thank goodness! Then what's the bad news?"

"You hain't never *had* a septic tank!"

"What?"

The septic tank inspection that we had paid for, and that showed clearly on our paperwork, proved that it had passed the investigation. The plumber was now repeating it again to reinforce his response. "I said there ain't no tank here."

It was just a hole dug in the ground with a steel lid laid on top. The dishonest owners had simply shoveled out a hole and installed flimsy landscape pipes to draw away excess sewer if the hole over-filled.

"So where does the runoff go if the hole overfills?" I hated to ask, but I had to know.

His answer, "It goes over them thar hill to the crick back of your house."

After the plumbers left, I phoned the county health department. I advised them of our predicament, and they sent out an agent to inspect our yard. He did a half-hearted inspection and, without performing a proper percolation (perc) test for water absorption, told us our only option was to install an expensive mound system. I took a deep breath. "What will your recommended type of tank cost?"

He seemed unconcerned as he replied, "You're looking at about $8,000 to $11,000." The worst news was that we had only ten days to find a suitable alternative for sewage disposal, or our home would be declared uninhabitable. We didn't have that kind of money.

In the past two years we had managed to squirrel away a little cash in hopes of using it for an attorney retainer fee. In the two years we had lived in the house, we had approached forty-two lawyers or law firms, hoping someone, anyone, would represent us in litigation against the former owners. Now, we had a difficult choice to make. We could put a down payment on a septic tank but have no money to begin our quest for justice, or we could continue trying to find an attorney and use a portable outhouse. It was a new setback for us, but we approached the problem in the same way we had handled our previous troubles. We knelt in prayer.

Within a few short days, He gave us the answer. It came by way of John, not a person, but a Porta-John. I had made phone calls throughout the valley and had finally found a company that would deliver to us an outhouse. It seemed a humorous correlation when we recognized that God was going to be the power behind our "throne."

Two days later we heard the beep, beep, beep warning of a large truck backing up our driveway. The piercing noise sounded like a garbage truck. I went out to see what it was and found that our newest home acquisition was being delivered. Our port-a-potty was a bright Smurf-blue. It was not nearly as attractive as we had hoped, if a port-a-potty could even be attractive. The driver unloaded it at the top of the driveway nearest our side door.

We were grateful that our little blue house couldn't be seen from the road below. If we needed to visit it during the night, it was situated in a way that no one would be able to see us in our pajamas. At the sight of it, my wife shrugged her shoulders and mumbled, "I wonder how long we'll be using this thing?" It was more of a statement than a question.

A few days following the delivery of our polyethylene and aluminum accented outhouse, we were greeted at our front door by my mother. My parents had just arrived from New England in order to spend the Thanksgiving holiday with us. "What in the world is that?" Her tone of voice conveyed her obvious disapproval. I provided my mother with a long and carefully worded explanation. Our bright blue port-a-potty was our new bathroom for the foreseeable future, I explained. Both of my parents were less than impressed.

The following day, we said our goodbyes. It had been the shortest visit they had ever made. Waving to them as they drove off, Le Anne jokingly remarked, "Wow, if I'd known it was this easy to keep guests from visiting, I would have gotten one of these things a long time ago."

Like every home, our little outhouse had its unpleasantries. During the winter it felt like a meat locker and in the summer, it was comparable to sitting on a park bench surrounded by molten lava, not to mention that certain uninviting "air" in the place. A recurring springtime annoyance was the relentless invasion of red wasps. They were tireless in their search for a place to build their nests, and for some reason, were overtly attracted to the outhouse. One year the wasp problem was so bad that we couldn't use the facility for two weeks or we would have surely gotten stung. Despite killing them by the dozens they kept swarming into our space. I had to inspect the "little blue house" often so our children wouldn't be fearful of using it.

One moonlit night, I took my flashlight along with me and paid a visit to, what I like to think of as, my second house. (My second house's monthly "mortgage" was $93.00 per month). As I pulled some paper off the roll, my inadequate light barely revealed a huge red wasp clinging to the middle of the sheet. He was not happy about being roused from his slumber. His antennae moved menacingly back and forth as if to warn me of impending consequences should I irritate him further. It didn't matter, because his doom was sealed. I quickly sent him to his final resting place below the blue-tinted water. I shuddered to think that had I not had my flashlight this night, I was one procedure away from thinking I had become a Christian with renewed enthusiasm.

On another summer evening I had an additional surprising encounter. As I sat down, I instantly regretted my decision. I felt a painful pinch. Thinking I had been jabbed by a wasp, I jumped up so fast that I tripped on my pant legs that were pooled around my ankles and fell out into the driveway. A graceful exit it was not! At least I had been spared the further indignity of anyone witnessing my disgraceful pratfall. To say my pride was wounded was an understatement. Humbled, I returned inside the blue shack to inspect the reason for my quick departure. It had not been a wasp that had pinched me after all – but a wonky toilet seat. This was going to take some getting used to.

One cold winter's night, I heard wild animals fighting in the woods beyond our driveway. Expecting to see something scurry away, I opened the outhouse door to discover a most breathtaking panorama of the night sky. The stars seemed exceptionally bright. As I looked at the constellation, Orion, I felt insignificant and small. Some have surmised that it is this very constellation where God sits on His heavenly throne. Now on my own "throne" gazing upward, I chuckled to myself that His seat was far more opulent than mine.

The outhouse served as an appointed detour during our journey to justice. With renewed urgency for God's intervention, and knowing scripture gives Jesus the title of Advocate, we persevered. In the five years we used our make-do restroom, we would pay for it many times over. As the rental fees would exceed over $5,600.

But God was faithful. After two years of searching, we found an attorney who took pity on our situation. He asked how much we could put down for a retainer, and we told him we had $5,000. He said it would be enough and agreed to take our case. Looking back, I'm certain that if he had known how long our case would be drawn out, he would never have accepted it. I give him credit for his enduring patience. He stuck with us as our case inched its way through the justice system, with the burden mostly on his shoulders.

Because the government was involved, our lawsuit languished in the courts for seven and a half years. Each time we thought we were close to a court date; we would have a disappointing delay. The government once postponed a trial date a full year because a witness claimed she couldn't testify as she had to babysit her out-of-state grandchildren. I lost my patience a few times when leaving our attorney's office over such drivel. It seemed the government was purposely stalling our case in order to persuade us to give up on it. Their ploys only hardened our resolve to see this saga through to its proper conclusion.

Patience was not one of my best virtues, but it was necessary for God to improve this quality in me. He wasn't ready for everything to be revealed yet. We would not try to hurry God. At this point, our patience was necessary because two future cataclysmic events would teach us to to fully place our trust in Him.

For Such a Call as This

"The Lord will fight for you, and you have only to be silent." Exodus 14:14 (ESV)

It was a typical fall day in Appalachia. The air was like the crisp bite of a freshly picked apple and was tinged with the fragrance of lingering firewood smoke. As the best weeks of autumn were approaching, it seemed a good time to celebrate the change of seasons. We had plans for a family picnic that day, but it would not prove to be a day for enjoyment. The serenity of our home was interrupted by the unwelcome ringing of the telephone.

I picked up the receiver and heard a woman's frail thin voice say, "Hello pastor." The voice was well-known to me. It was one of my church members whose health was failing. Though she was only in her late forties, her incurable illness had made her body look as if she were twice her age. She was gaunt, and the pallor of her skin was an indication of the cruel progression of her illness.

"Hello," I responded.

As calm and collected as if she were discussing the weather, she blurted out a question. "Will you do my funeral?"

Knowing her illness had worsened recently, and fearing she was giving up hope, I replied, "Of course, but why ask me now?"

"Because you're going to have to do it this weekend."

I knew that she had a husband and a teenage son to worry about, and up until now, it was this family that had strengthened her will to live. I sensed that her situation was not as dire as she was portraying. In fact, I thought she was one of those people who had become addicted to her misery. I quickly asked her if she had told her husband what she had just told me. She had not and went on to say that it was her decision, and nothing was going to stop her. Adding to the drama of her announcement, she punctuated it by hanging up on me.

Thinking that maybe she had really given up, I grew alarmed. I franticly dialed her number, but there was no answer. Concerned that she would try to end her life, if her husband and son were not at home, I sprang into action. I didn't want our conversation to be our last. I quickly called her personal physician, who was a mutual friend of both of ours, and relayed to him what had just transpired. His quick assessment was the same as mine: an intervention was needed – immediately. I anxiously called a second friend who was a crisis counselor. After hearing the details of the situation, he too agreed that immediate assistance was needed.

From my years as a healthcare administrator, I followed what I knew to be proper protocol. I called my ministerial boss in Nashville and quickly recounted the events. He rapidly approved my request to seek help for my church member and asked to be kept updated.

Next, I notified the police department in the woman's small town and explained my concerns. The officer I spoke to was direct.

"Does she have a weapon?"

I thought this question was inane. I countered with a question of my own. "What woman in Appalachia *doesn't* have a gun?"

He hesitated as he thought over my remark. "Well then, we'll meet you there and wait until you arrive."

Fearing her life could at that moment be slipping away, I gave the officer her address and rushed out to my car. Would she follow through on her threat? I drove as fast as I could during the thirty-mile drive; I was fortunate that no highway patrol caught me speeding.

As I arrived at her house on the top of a hill, a police officer exited his patrol car and approached me. Hurriedly, I apprised him of the situation, and we knocked on the front door. The officer was standing behind me when we heard the woman's feeble voice answer, "Come in."

As we entered her cramped stuffy living room, we found her sitting alone on the couch. In the dimly lit room, she looked heartbroken and forlorn. I walked toward her and leaned down to speak with her. "You had me feeling so scared. Why did you make such a self-threatening call?" I asked. To make better eye contact, I knelt down in front of her. Just as I did, she glanced over my shoulder and realized that a uniformed police officer was standing in her doorway. Unmistakable outrage immediately flashed across her face. Her voice somehow gathered strength.

"Why did you bring *him* here? How dare you do that to me! What will the neighbors think!" She began to tremble as torrents of her long-held bitterness gushed out like a flood. I tried to calm her down by redirecting the conversation.

"Why didn't you answer the phone when I called you back?" Now seeing her husband out of the corner of my eye, I didn't wait for her to answer. "Why didn't you tell me your husband was here in the house?"

She never answered the question and, at that point, lost control and shrieked, "You betrayed me!"

I tried to reassure her that because I cared for her, I was willing to risk the loss of her friendship, especially if it meant that she wouldn't harm herself. I asked her about her teenage son, trying to get her to think about what it would be like for him, if he had come home from school and found his mother dead. She would have none of that tactic, and began to rant at us, demanding that we both leave immediately. Oddly, her husband stepped back into the shadows of the kitchen, saying nothing.

The police officer, losing patience with her belligerent behavior, gave a harsh warning. "Look lady, we're here to help. If you keep up this attitude, I can throw you in the loony bin!"

I was taken aback. As I turned to the officer, and gave him my best, I-can't-believe-you- just-said-that look, his face hardened, and he forcefully demanded "Ma'am put the weapon down!"

I swung around to see that, while my back was turned, she had pulled out a pistol from between the couch cushions. Shaking with rage, she was aiming the gun directly at us. I was positioned in front of the officer, and with one shot, I knew that she could hit both of us. The first thought that flashed into my mind was, *I wonder if she's a good markswoman*. From the frenzied look fixed on her face, we knew her threat was real.

Slowly, quietly, we backed out the front door.

Back on the front porch, we stepped away from the door and window, lest she were to see us. The officer immediately called for backup. His ill-timed and offensive remark had churned up my indignation. As soon as he finished his call, I confronted him.

"Why would you goad her like that? You didn't have to tell her you would throw her in the "loony bin!"

Shaking his finger at me, he retorted, "Look, I'm protecting myself from getting shot. I have a family to go home to!"

Within minutes, the woman's small rural street was cordoned off by the town's entire police force. Four additional patrol cars, plus the arriving chief of police, were now at the scene. The neighbors began gathering on their porches. This was as good as it could get – just like a real police action TV show. The chief motioned with his arm for the neighbors to go back inside. He was unsuccessful. They were determined not to miss any of this unfolding drama.

The situation began to feel more urgent as the officers stationed themselves on either side of the woman's house. Hands on their guns, they waited. After speaking with his first officer, the chief then made his way toward me. He wanted to know what the woman was like, the state of her physical condition, and if I had her phone number. I gave him all her information, and then he asked if he could use my cellphone.

I dialed the number and promptly handed him the phone. She wouldn't answer. He redialed. On the fourth attempt, she relented. He identified himself and asked if he could come inside. From where I was standing, I heard her agitated, and suddenly powerful, voice shout into the phone, "No!" Then she hung up.

As we waited from a distance, she walked out to her front porch, revolver still in hand, and began to exhibit further erratic behavior. I had never seen her act in such a way. She smoked several cigarettes and paced warily like a cornered animal. As if she were being hunted, her eyes darted back and forth between the officers crouching at the corners of her house and her neighbors who were now growing more inquisitive. Everyone was intently focused on her every move.

The chief called out to her in his best calming voice. "Please, I only want to talk to you and hear your grievance. Let's go inside and chat." After much wavering, she agreed to allow him entry, but with the stipulation that he leave his weapon behind. She also demanded that he promise not to throw her in an asylum, as the first officer had threatened.

Having gained her trust, he handed his sidearm to one of his officers and cautiously proceeded toward the front door. Motioning to his team, he gave them signals as to how he wanted to proceed. They would rush in when prompted. About ten minutes passed after he had entered the house, but to those outside, wondering if they would hear a gunshot, it seemed much longer.

I learned later, that when the chief entered her house, he had squatted down at her eye level in order to gain her trust. It was in that position that he could quickly swat away her gun, if it were still in her hands. From the sidelines, the woman's husband encouraged her to follow the chief's direction. As the chief continued his soothing small talk, she felt less threatened. Beginning to relax her grip on the weapon, she lowered the barrel. The chief knew this was his moment to gain control.

He lunged forward to restrain her, giving his signal to the waiting officers. In a coordinated fashion, they stormed through the front door and each grabbed one her flailing limbs. Consumed with rage at being deceived by the chief, she gave them all a vociferous tongue-lashing, in the worst possible terms. I had never before seen one of my church members kicking, screaming, and shouting obscenities. The call was made for an ambulance, and soon we heard the wail of the siren coming down the street.

Strapped to a gurney, with her arms restrained at her sides, she was taken out to the waiting emergency vehicle. The EMTs advised her husband and me that she would be evaluated at the local hospital's psychiatric unit. At most, her stay would last four or five days.

Realizing her fate as the ambulance doors were closing, she released what little venom she had left for me. Lifting her head from the pillow she screamed, "I hate you!" The ambulance sped off, with its lights flashing.

The neighbors returned to their homes, and the woman's husband and I sat down on the concrete steps of the front porch. He thanked me. "I'm so glad you got her some help. She's needed it for a long time. If I had called, she would have gotten so angry that she would have divorced me." He went on to express his gratitude that she was now safe. We prayed together, and as I prepared to leave, I asked him to keep me updated on his wife's condition. He assured me that he would.

As I drove home, I felt utterly drained. I wondered how the other church members would react *if* the news of this trouble were to be leaked. I hoped for the woman's sake that her husband would keep it quiet.

The next day I conducted a regular service at one of the three churches, as if nothing had happened. While on the drive home one of the leaders of the church, where the family regularly attended, phoned. He began with, "Did you hear what happened at church today?"

Feeling butterflies start to hatch in my stomach, I responded, "No, what happened?"

He went on to relate that during the prayer request portion of the service, the woman's husband had woven quite the tale. I listened to his unhappy description of the church's reaction to the husband's story. That segment of the service had been inappropriately turned from praise and prayer requests into a gossip session. The leader's assessment of what had transpired broke my heart.

In a desperate attempt to show his own importance and recognition, the woman's husband had stunned the church with the words, "Please pray for my wife. She called the pastor for help and he had her committed!" Gasps of disbelief and surprise had pulsed through the room. The day's sermon was no longer important. Seeds of anger were taking root.

As I listened to the leader, I became bewildered. How could the husband, not twenty-four hours earlier, thank me, and then tell his church that I (his pastor) had betrayed his wife? I knew that in Florida, the process of having a person committed to a psychiatric unit was done under a law known as The Baker Act, but this was Appalachia, and that was only an unfortunate name coincidence. It seemed the members hadn't realized that a pastor was not allowed to have someone committed – only a doctor or civil authority could do that.

A quote that is attributed to Charles Spurgeon, (and others,) came to my mind as I drove. Now I understood its meaning: "A lie can travel halfway around the world while the truth is pulling on its shoes."

My leader's voice jolted me back to the conversation, "The church is up in arms and they are really angry at you. They can't believe you could treat someone this way."

Three days later, the fallout from the incident became noticeable at prayer meeting. I could sense by the members' cold reception that this situation was going to become much more difficult; they were in no mood for prayer or a meeting. Later, as my wife and I lay in bed that night, we prayed that God would give me wisdom to handle the situation and the right opportunity to explain the truth. Despite the unfairness of being personally assailed each day for weeks, God's plan would not be rushed.

Developing patience was becoming a central theme in the early days of our ministry. As each new challenge was thrust upon us, it tested our resolve. One week turned into two, two into four. Yet, through the tempest we remained silent and continued to pray. Calls for legal action, and threats of a letter-writing campaign to have us ousted, sprang up. I knew the truth was going to exonerate me, but when would God allow me the opportunity to set the record straight? It had been six weeks since the sad event, and our acceptance among the members was at its lowest point.

One morning, while in prayer, God impressed upon me that it was time. After breakfast I drove back to the woman's town to request a copy of the police report. It was public record now, and I was confident that my request would be approved. At the police station, I spoke to the dispatcher, and in just a few minutes, she provided the documentation I needed. With proof in hand, my quest for absolution could begin. The following Saturday I advised the church that an important announcement would be made at prayer meeting. I told them "You won't want to miss it."

The crowd that gathered the following Wednesday night was larger than usual. Every member was in attendance except for two, a man and his wife who, many times before, had both been gossiping and fanning the flames of discontent. The suspense in the room was almost palpable. Whispering began in anticipation of what was going to be announced. Would I be giving up my position as pastor, or would I try to justify my past actions? I opened our meeting with prayer and petitioned God to give us understanding and wisdom.

The members I stood before were not from the same church where the woman had threatened to take her own life yet, oddly, they were the church that had given me the greatest challenge over the incident. I took a deep breath and began, "How many of you here have heard about an event in our church district that involved an individual who had threatened suicide?" Each of them shook their head to indicate no. I continued, "As pastor, it's my duty to maintain and defend the dignity and confidentiality of every member. Over the past six weeks I have done that. Now because of loose lips and gossiping, the only person's dignity that must be defended is mine."

I proceeded to read out the four counts listed on the police report. The woman had been charged with wanton endangerment, assaulting a police officer, menacing (displaying a weapon with intent to make another person be in fear of injury or death), and pointing a loaded gun at a police officer. When I finished reading the charges, murmurs were heard, and objections were promptly raised. "That's not what we heard!" It would have been comical if the meeting had not been so serious. Just moments before, they had all indicated that they knew nothing of the incident!

I passed the report to them for verification. At this point, they already knew the woman's name. As the truth of the event was made known, the room became oddly quiet. Was the awkward silence due to regret and remorse for doubting the word of their pastor? The lesson learned that night had been effective and powerful. Gossip, the most destructive of scourges, destroys relationships and trust, both in churches and in families.

The following weekend, while I was away, the gossiping troublemaker and his wife, who had been conspicuously absent from the previous meeting, made their appearance at church. They had come to invite the members to leave with them and start another church! Unaware that their audience was now in possession of the true story, the couple became confused. The members were now in *support* of their pastor, instead of wanting him to leave. Disgraced and defeated, the two left–never to return.

Their bitterness and anger took a toll on their health. Just six months after their dramatic departure, the husband developed career-ending contractures of his hands and his wife developed cancer. Rebellion against God has serious consequences. Several additional events, in the years ahead, gave credence to our church members, that God had *indeed* called us to serve them there. We were, in this season of time, His ambassadors.

"But to you who are listening I say: Love your enemies, do good to those who hate you, bless those who curse you, pray for those who mistreat you." Luke 6:27-28 (NIV)

The "Doggone" Tarp

"Amazed and perplexed, they asked one another,
"What does this mean?" Acts 2:12 (NIV)

It was once again late May and time for our family to make the required annual trek to Tennessee for the denomination's old-time campmeeting. It always concerned me when I had to leave my home unattended for the two-week period. What would I find when I returned? Would we break another water line? Would a pipe break? Would the hot water spring a leak and ruin all the floors? And why did the lawn seem to grow so wildly when we are absent? The grass would grow so tall it seemed I needed a pith helmet and safari elephant to find my front door when we returned.

Then there were snakes that were drawn to the tall grass. While we hadn't seen any of the poisonous varieties, we had been visited by Black Racers, Eastern Hog-nosed, and Milk snakes. My wife was insistent that I search the internet prior to killing any snake in our yard. I tried to convince her that the snake in question would be long gone before I could identify it, but she was adamant. My admonitions to the snakes to stay put, until I could find out whether or not they were poisonous were never successful.

As our departure date drew near, I began worrying about all the things that might go wrong at the house. I set interventions and plans into place on the remote chance that any of those conditions would occur. I should have known better than to try, because plans can be like hospital gowns: you foolishly think that you have more coverage than you really do.

The day before we were to leave, a big yellow truck drove up our hill and parked in our driveway. It was a tree-trimming crew who worked for our local power company. They had come to request our permission to do, as the foreman described it, "a little bit of trimming on the trees near your powerlines." Since our yard and above-ground pool were safely hidden behind a lush wall of green growth, I granted them permission, but with the caveat that they only do a light trimming–not a major cutting. We loved the privacy that the foliage afforded us–it blocked our pool from prying eyes. The foreman added that we would be the last house that week to have it done.

The next day we loaded up our car for the five-hour drive. After a short prayer for safe travelling, we headed out. Our family dog Goldie, a sweet "Heinz 57" rescue, watched forlornly from the front yard. Not allowed to attend, she had to be left behind, with a promise from a friend to check on her. She equally despised any kind of chain, collar, or strap. Like Houdini, she was an expert at getting out of them. Because of her prowess to escape, we would have to leave her unrestrained but happy to roam about the hills and hollers.

The two weeks of meetings went by relatively fast. As we expected when we returned home, our lawn had the appearance of the Amazon. What we weren't prepared for was the devastation left behind by the electric company's trimmers. Our hearts

The "Doggone" Tarp

sank when we saw that the top of every majestic pine tree along our road had been sliced off. Our formerly lovely trees had been reduced to blunted stumps. By the pool, all of our beautiful vines had been chopped away. Our privacy wall of foliage was obliterated. We were livid when we saw tree limbs and debris littering our four hundred feet of road frontage. To make matters worse, the crew had left a note on our side entrance door. Thinking it was to let us know about the trees, I picked it up. It simply read: you have a dead dog in your pool.

Our own dog Goldie was overjoyed to see us and bounded up as soon as we had returned. So, whose dog could it be? Feeling some consternation, I walked around the corner of the house to our backyard pool. I was not prepared for the overpowering stench. A neighbor's white furry dog had somehow made its way out on top of our yet-to-be-uncovered pool. Unable to climb off the wet and sagging tarp, it had promptly died. During our absence the temperatures had been in the low nineties, and guessing by the state of the animal's remains, it had lain there for about that long.

When the children saw what was on the sagging tarp, and took in the putrid odor, they all pronounced in unison, "Ewwwww… that's gross!" Using the long handle of my shovel to keep the heavy waterlogged canine at arms -length, I draped the carcass evenly over the end, and carried it gingerly to the end of our property for disposal.

My next challenge was to restore our pool back to its pristine state. I contacted a pool company and told them about our predicament. They suggested using four packages of super shock powder, and afterwards retest the water. Easy enough, I thought.

Since the pool cover was still intact, I didn't want to risk getting any of the dog's remains into the pool itself. I dumped the powder on to the place where the dog had lain. The resulting chemical reaction took on the appearance of an eighth-grade baking soda and vinegar volcano demonstration. As the powder combined with the organic matter, it created a boiling cauldron effect. Churning water, teeming with tufts of fur, bubbled up with abandon.

In an instant, I was able to accomplish something I'd never be able to replicate. I had surpassed my children's gross-out factor times ten. They yelled, "Yuck! Gross! That's disgusting!" As they ran back into the house, they swore they would never swim in the pool again.

The next day, I pulled off the pool cover in order to clean away the chemical residue. I hung it up by its straps and went to retrieve the garden hose. It was then that I had an "aha" moment. It was similar to finding something mundane that resembled something important. It was as if I had discovered some condensation on a window at Christmastime that looked exactly like the shape of Santa Claus.

This time, the caricature's resemblance was real! Our blue pool cover now displayed a dog's full profile, permanently etched into its fibers. It was quite reminiscent of a chalk outline at a crime scene. The silhouette was impressive. Tail, ears, and legs were perfectly rendered in a bleached-out silhouette on a background of blue. It was at this point that I mused to myself; the cover should have been used for a twenty-five-foot flag over a pet superstore. Toni was unimpressed. "Oh daddy," she wailed. "It's too horrible; pleeeeeze buy a new one!"

As I followed the process of restoring the integrity of the water, I thought that the contents of the pool basket looked like a goat that had been pureed in the blender. I persevered, and after five days of removing fur and debris, my work was complete. The water was so pristine it could have sanitized surgical instruments. But she wasn't so sure; she still refused to swim the rest of that summer.

By season's end, the ongoing mystery was what further passed through that pool skimmer basket. I took the attitude that some mysteries were better left unsolved. Around our house, we no longer use the phrase, "the dog days of summer." That "ruff" patch is still too fresh in our minds.

Lessons from Tall Tales

"The Lord will keep you from all harm—he will watch over your life; the Lord will watch over your coming and going both now and forevermore." Psalm 121:7,8 (NIV)

I have no idea why my presence attracts interesting characters. It doesn't matter where I am traveling–in America, Canada, or Italy–the outcome is always the same. A person will shuffle up to me, and within minutes, their life story of woe and affliction will be proclaimed–from sand flea bites to lumbago. They will announce that a family member has just died, their pickup truck needs a battery, or they are in desperate need of a hotel for "just one night." They claim they are on their way east while oddly heading in the opposite direction.

One night, I was meeting with one of my church members at a local donut shop. My personal magnetism must have been at full drawing power, for no sooner had we sat down for a quick snack then a disheveled-looking couple, in their late thirties, approached me. Tearfully, they relayed their story of woe and then requested a ride to pay respects to a close family member who had just died. Due to our unspoken suspicions, my church

Lessons from Tall Tales

friend did not want me to travel alone with this couple. As his car was full of books, it was agreed that he would drive behind me in order to keep his eyes on the situation. The intended destination was a funeral home fifteen miles away.

As I drove, the bedraggled man sat in the front seat, and his shabbily dressed girlfriend in the back. Endeavoring to break the awkward silence, or perhaps to gain some personal respect, the man announced that he had served in Vietnam. Surprised, I said, "You appear a little too young to have served in Vietnam."

With a sideways glance he countered, "Well, I didn't fight in the first war; I fought in the second one." That was my first clue that this was going to be a memorable and outlandish ride.

As we drove, he spoke in an adamant voice to the woman that they should have the money ready to give to the funeral home when they arrived. The woman responded by whining that she couldn't find it. In exasperation, and with a thick southern twang, he responded urgently, "Baby, check your braww!"

As if she was digging for turnips, the woman partially disrobed and began probing with her hands to find the missing money wedged somewhere in her undergarment. I've prayed for many things but asking God to help find money in her bra (and fast) was a new one for me. I'm convinced that it must have been a new one for God too. Moments later, with a triumphant shout, she announced that her personal scavenger hunt was over. Secure in this good news, my hitchhiker in the front seat mumbled a few words of acknowledgement, slumped over against the passenger window, and began to snooze.

As we drew close to their requested destination, I glanced in my rearview mirror to make sure that my church member was still behind me – thank goodness he was. Slowly waking up, my male passenger instructed me to turn down a dark narrow street with several abandon brick buildings. The funeral home's location they sought was obviously nowhere in sight. They told me to stop the car and asked me to wait for them. The establishment they went in to, lacking dignity, looked more like a "happening place." Every light was on. As my church friend and I waited patiently in our cars, I began to feel uneasy. This was no ordinary house. Each person that entered, or departed it, stared at us like we were Communist insurgents. Those going inside would only stay about ten to fifteen minutes, then as they left, we would receive their glaring stares again.

I didn't think that I looked suspicious. I was only driving a white Mercury Grand Marquis. Then I had a flash of insight. Weren't most unmarked police cars the *same* as mine? After making that connection, the glaring stares made sense. In all likelihood, my friend and I were parked right in front of a drug house. To those inside, it must have appeared that we were undercover cops!

Grabbing my cellphone, I urgently called my church member in order to warn him about where we were. His phone was turned off. Not wanting to risk getting out of my car, I rolled down the window and yelled to him, "Don't get out of your car!"

"What?" He shouted back.

I yelled at him again, "Whatever you do, don't get out of your car!"

"Okay," he responded.

Just as I was deciding it was time to leave our dishonest couple behind, I was interrupted by a tapping on my window. As I rolled it down, my church friend leaned over and asked, "What did you say?"

With irritation I warned, "I said, don't get out of your car, it's not safe here. We need to leave immediately!"

"Oh. Okay." He lumbered back to his idling car. Seconds later he was back, rapping on my window again.

Clearly exasperated, I snapped "What now?"

"Um…I've locked my keys in the car."

It was then that I noticed the couple was walking back to my car. The man demanded, "We want you to take us to another place." Unpersuaded, I gritted my teeth and responded "Sorry, we have to wait here for the auto club." Saying that they couldn't hold on, they walked away into the enclosing darkness and disappeared from my view.

While we waited for the auto club to arrive, I began to pray and watch my surroundings incessantly. Shadowy figures would slowly approach our vehicles. In an effort to cast some light on the area, I would depress the brake pedal, and the figures would slip furtively away. This process was repeated numerous times.

One interminable hour later after umpteen times of playing our version of the children's game, Red-Light Green-Light, the auto club truck arrived. It was the first time I had ever seen the AAA arrive in an unidentified, beat-up vehicle. The driver cautiously approached my car and inquired, "What in the world are you doing out here at this hour?"

I retorted flippantly, "We were hungry and looking for Girl Scout Cookies."

Looking over his shoulder he shook his head, "You won't find any in *this* neighborhood, especially at one a.m."

After regaining entry to his car, my friend and I, having learned some valuable lessons, headed home. God had protected us, despite our naiveté. In the future, we would not be visiting donut shops after ten p.m.

Despite my prior lapses of good judgement, my learning curve with people seeking assistance began to improve. As the treasurer of the county ministerial association, I frequently found myself receiving calls for monetary help. One day a request came by way of a concerned mother whose daughter and grandchild were at risk of having their electricity shut off.

A co-worker and I got the address for the daughter, and when we arrived, we proceeded up a metal staircase leading into a second story apartment above a filling station. The woman was an impeccable housekeeper, and her toddler was nicely dressed and clean. Sitting down on her sofa, she began to tell us why she was in her present circumstances. She had a low-paying job, her husband lived far away, and unexpected expenses had caused her meager bank account to dwindle. "Where is your husband?" I asked. With a sad expression, she hung her head and told us that he was serving a prison sentence in a western state. She hadn't seen him for two years.

Trying to be helpful, I offered, "We would never ask you to end your marriage, but if you were to file for a legal separation, your monthly benefits would increase. It would temporarily help with your financial situation."

With great conviction she gasped and said, "I would never do that. I believe strongly in my marriage commitment and in staying together!"

I was convinced she wasn't telling the truth, and let her response go unanswered. Her lack of veracity was obvious; how could she say that she believed so strongly in the sanctity of her marriage while keeping a straight face? The baby bump she was carrying showed that she was at least seven months pregnant. I'm not a doctor, but I'm most confident that babies aren't byproducts of pen-pal relationships. For the returning husband one day, I'm afraid this special delivery will require a signature of receipt – most likely that of an attorney.

God, Family, and Hand Sanitizer

> "But the Lord said to Samuel... The Lord does not look at the things people look at. People look at the outward appearance, but the Lord looks at the heart." 1 Samuel 16:7 (NIV)

There are many things in life that offer me security: God, my Bible, family, a place to call home, and hand sanitizer. God is always first. As for the rest they are not consistently listed in that descending order. Occasionally, I overdo the use of hand sanitizer–depending on the circumstances. Hand sanitizer, for me, is the "quintessence of life." It may be that its protective properties are no better than your teenaged son taking your car on his first date and saying, "Don't worry, Dad." But, I'm happy to slather it on anyway, even if it only offers me a smidgen of security; for as the common wisdom goes, "It's better than nothing."

My father once gave me some advice. He said, "If you're looking for a guarantee in life, then buy a toaster." He was correct in that he meant there were no real guarantees. Still, I like to think my hand disinfectant, (that closely resembles a can of gooey jellied Sterno) comes very close.

As For Me and My Out House,

    The local ministerial association I volunteered for had provided the address of another family in need. To determine a family's situation, I would often pay a personal visit before any money was dispersed. Often, my wife would accompany me and today was one of those days. We soon found the small white house. I should note that it *used* to be white, but most of the paint had faded away, and patches of splintering wood were now showing through. The trim was damaged and parts of it were missing.

    As we entered the front door, we couldn't help but notice that the house was dark and dingy. It was a warm and sunny day, but little light was being allowed in. As evidenced by the pitiful and sparse furniture in the living room, this family had fallen on hard times. The stained and dirty couch had three broken-off legs; propping it up were three grey cement blocks. There was a small television on a rickety stand, a grubby playpen in the corner of the room, and a sink full of dirty dishes. The interior of the rest of the house was an untidy wreck. The woman, who welcomed us inside, was a mother of four children ranging in ages from eighteen months to twenty-two years. Her hair was unwashed and as greasy as if she had just rubbed Vaseline on it. She was unkempt and looked exhausted.

    As we sat down on the make-do couch, her toddler cried out for attention. He wanted to be taken out of his playpen, now that interesting guests were present. While I tried to speak with his mother, the child's wailing grew louder. In exasperation, the woman turned to my wife and in a pleading voice said, "Would you hold him for me?" She lifted up the grubby-faced child so he could run toward Le Anne's outstretched arms. Once the toddler was seated on her lap, my wife remarked with surprise. "Oh, he's wet from head to toe."

His mother replied wistfully, "Yeah, he loves playing in the toilet. We can't keep him out of it." Wide-eyed with horror, my wife conveyed her immediate feelings to me. It was an unspoken request for hand sanitizer! Our visit became a very quick one.

After filling the needy family's request, and saying a prayer for them, we made a beeline for our car. As we walked down the front porch steps, my wife kept her soggy arms extended out in front of her. To her credit, we always carry a giant tub of pump-action hand sanitizer in our car. Thank heaven for its germicidal power!!!

Later that same week, I received a call from one of my church leaders. A family that we had not seen for ages needed a visit. We agreed on a rendezvous time and place then proceeded to follow directions to the family's home. We were unprepared for driving on the treacherous back road to their house. The mile and a half drive should only have been undertaken by military jeep. Twice we stopped to pray that God would help us to pass over the cavernous three-bedroom-two- bath ruts. During the drive to their house we were glad that speed was not essential, for we were travelling at the pace of a person-pulled rickshaw.

As the woodland road opened into a wide clearing, we saw a ramshackle two-bay garage in an open field. Getting out of our car, we realized that the building was surrounded by what appeared to be a defunct junkyard. We made our way cautiously around mounds of rusting car parts, mangy-looking feral cats, and snarling dogs. There was not a section of the property that was without debris. Tentatively, we approached the side entrance door.

Surprised that they had visitors, the family eagerly invited us into their one room garage home. I marveled at how a family of four, including a teenaged son and daughter, could live his way. The walls were bare except for some holes that filtered in light from the outside. The stifling summer heat made the interior of their shelter almost unbearable. When I saw their simple kerosene heater located in a corner, I wondered how they were able to endure the frigid Appalachian winters. The hardship of their lives was reflected in the mother's appearance. She clearly looked at least twenty years older than her actual age.

During the course of our conversation, I asked about her husband. She responded that he had finally found a job in town and how their lives had improved. I remember thinking… improved from what? "My husband's work is only about fifteen miles away," She proudly announced.

I considered their pitiful home, the piles of junk in the yard, and the hazardous entrance road. I asked, "Why don't you move closer to town for his job?" She gasped, and with a sweeping arm motion exclaimed, as if referring to paradise, "What, and leave all this?"

As my church member and I made our way back to my car, we once again maneuvered our way around used transmissions and what looked like scavenged heaps of space junk. Lost in our own thoughts, we hardly spoke during our arduous ride out to the main road.

In the past, I had worked with individuals who had lost their sight, but for this woman's unique kind of "blindness," I had not been prepared. I petitioned the Lord as we drove home, "Make me as oblivious to the challenges and obstacles in my life, as this woman is to the rubble that surrounds her." God had lifted away my own perceptual prejudice. It was a lesson I would never forget.

"Deerly" Departed

"The righteous person may have many troubles, but the LORD delivers him from them all."
Psalm 34:19 (NIV)

The larger-than-normal church district we managed stretched along the borders of three states and sixteen counties. That meant during the year we would spend a quarter of every month's salary on gas. We were driving fifty to sixty thousand miles annually! Driving that many miles meant that we had a better than average chance of vehicle mishaps. My wife and I daily asked God to provide a hedge of protection around us as we drove. Additionally, with the assistance of two church members who owned a car repair business, we felt we were covered.

One day, our Nissan's fan blower sounded like it had something trapped inside of its vents. When the fan was turned on, it produced a brushing sound like that of a baseball card pinned to a bicycle spoke. Click-clack click-clack. As a child, it was a fun distraction, but as an adult on a long drive, the noise was annoying. I called my friends at the repair shop, and they told me to bring my car to them on Wednesday. What they found, brought us all a hearty laugh.

Apparently, my garage was home to some mice that had found refuge under the hood of my car. This fact was revealed when the vehicle was placed on the lift at the shop and the cover of the fan was removed. Like an unrolling party favor, a long snakeskin dropped down out of the box toward one of the mechanics. With a yell of surprise, the man jumped back. It soon became apparent that a large snake had chased a mouse into the blower motor assembly, and once twisted inside it, had eaten the unfortunate rodent. Like someone unfastening their pants button after a large meal, the snake had wriggled out of its skin and called it a day. I can't recall the price of the "repair." But it wouldn't surprise me to learn that an extra five dollars had been tacked on to accommodate the purchase of a new pair of undershorts for the technician.

In the Appalachian animal kingdom, I had to have been a feared legend. During our nine-year tenure, I had either hit, or almost hit every known animal species in the region. I nearly lost my car's oil pan one night to an armored possum – the armadillo. That encounter made quite the racket. On another night after prayer meeting, a majestic elk, with an impressive rack of antlers, was suddenly standing in the road. He was dazzled by my headlights, and I missed him by mere inches.

Despite all of my precautionary driving skills, one animal species became a recurring nemesis for me: the all-too-frequent deer. We were on our way to a church meeting one winter's night, when a doe chose to cut directly in front of our fast-travelling car. I slammed on my brakes. My reaction time was good, but there was not enough room to stop. We heard the alarming screech of tires on the road, followed by the thunderous bang. The doe bounced off the front of the car, turned completely around in midair, then skidded across the road to end up in a shallow ditch.

The night air was icy as I got out of the car to survey the damage. I shook my head in disbelief. This was our fourth deer collision in six years. Both headlights and the hood of our car were smashed and mangled, the grill was barely hanging on, the radiator was spewing steam, and the hood ornament was missing.

In a quirk of timing, a pickup truck drove up beside us. Being the first driver at the scene of our accident, I expected that he would ask us if we were all right. I was mistaken. Apparently, he did not care. Seeing the condition of our car, he surmised that we must have hit a deer. He had only one question, "Has the deer been dead long?"

Tongue-in-cheek I snapped, "No, you're in luck. It's fresh off the grill."

Missing the pun, he looked around and made his way over to the ditch. Picking the doe up by the legs, he heaved it into the back of his pickup bed. The adage that "one man's loss is another man's gain," was the summary of our misfortune that night. With a quick wave of his hand, the man drove away happy, as if he had won the road-kill lottery.

I made the call to the auto club and requested a tow truck. My wife was impressed that I had remembered the number for AAA. "Are you kidding? I have their number on speed dial!"

Despite our setback, God was providing for us. We were within towing range for car repairs, and some church friends picked us up, and offered us a place for the night.

As our heads "hit the pillows," we were grateful. This appointed "de(er)tour" came with a comfortable bed and kind friends.

When you live a life completely built on faith, you become attuned to recognizing all manner of blessing, large or small – even when people and nature collide.

The Phoenix Miracle

> "Now to him who is able to do immeasurably more than all we ask or imagine, according to his power that is at work within us, to him be glory in the church and in Christ Jesus throughout all generations, for ever and ever! Amen." Ephesians 3:21,21 (NIV)

It was tough making visits to our attorney's office knowing that each time would no doubt be just another excuse and delay. For us, we relied on prayer and humor to get us through. One such day as we entered our attorney's office, he heard us laughing before we entered. Our lighthearted banter was always a conundrum for him as we dealt with one setback after another. He knew we were frustrated, yet as we entered his office and sat down, he blurted out, "You two always seem so happy, what's the secret of your marriage?"

I responded quickly "That's easy, we're never going to get divorced!"

With his eyebrow raised he asked, "How can you be so sure?"

"Because," I responded glibly, "no one wants the house!"

His hearty laugh set the tone for our update, but it was useless; little had changed since our last visit. Four years of setbacks, endless litigation, coupled with some renegade church members, our marriage and ministry still had to be our focus. With that in mind, we were apprised shortly thereafter of a pastor's marriage conference occurring in Arizona. We obtained permission and booked the trip. It would be two-fold; we would gain the necessary skills in building strong marriages and family relationships, and we could see family and friends who lived in the conference area.

Some years before, on a business trip to New England, we had experienced a credit card nightmare. The card kept being denied even though our expenditures were well within the card's limits. To keep this from happening and inconveniencing us again, we secured a brand-new credit card just for this trip. As we arrived for our first hotel stay, we used the credit card for the very first time. With a credit limit exceeding $1000, we were confident it would meet all our needs. We had never traveled anywhere where some stressful problem hadn't arisen, and it felt good that for the first time this trip would be different.

My wife is the first person to admit that I love getting a bargain. The hotel membership club we belonged to promised every second stay would garner a free third night. With a four-day conference, that meant we'd receive two hotel nights free to use as we chose at a later time. However, my frugality would serve as a source of frequent frustration for my wife as we had to pack and repack each day.

The first night had us in a nice well-kept establishment near the airport. The next night, as we entered the next hotel's lobby, a surprise awaited us. When we endeavored to check in after a long day of meetings, the front desk clerk told us our credit card had been declined. I said that was impossible; its brand new. The front desk clerk attempted to charge the card again, but it failed a second time.

As my wife patiently waited in a lobby easy chair, I called the credit card issuer to find out why the next charges been declined. The customer service representative was matter of fact, "You maxed it out at the Tempe Mall." "In fact," she went on, "Your wife just bought shoes today to the tune of $700 at one store."

Aghast, I responded, "there clearly is a mistake, if my wife spent $700 on shoes today, we'd be in marriage counseling right now!"

She chuckled a little and said she would refer these unauthorized charges to their fraud department. I, however, was not amused. She then bluntly stated, "I'm sorry, but your card is now null and void."

A fraud investigator told us later that the previous hotel receptionist must have been part of a credit card theft ring. It was a sophisticated operation because they took the numbers from our card, made their own credit card, then promptly maxed it out the very next day before getting caught.

We only had enough cash to pay the second hotel stay, but we would clearly need some help from my employer by way of an advance to finish the trip. My wife quickly but calmly reminded me that the devil's purpose is to steal our joy and keep us from getting the blessing we came for. With conviction and optimism in her voice, she said, "Let's make the best of it until we can get this fixed, and let God handle the rest."

All I could envision at this point was sitting by the side of the road with a cardboard sign that read, "Hungry" and an arrow pointing to the word Kentucky. The following day, my bosses came through with an emergency cash advance and we were able to attend the remainder of the marriage conference with greater peace.

The conference was riveting. We sat spellbound during the closing meeting when a young woman gave her testimony. She told a packed auditorium how her Christian marriage had withstood an affair that she had initiated. She had longed for attention from her busy husband and in a moment of weakness, she had fallen for the charms of a man who lavished her with attention. It was a onetime affair, but her lack of restraint had resulted in her becoming pregnant.

While harboring this secret from her husband, she told us all how her remorse was more than she could bear. She had been brought up in a good Christian home and knew her only true option was keeping the baby or giving it up for adoption. The audience sat with rapt attention as she bravely told of her tearful confession, she had made first to her Dad as he accompanied her to the doctor's office. Her father, a devout follower of Christ, gave her words of comfort that brought tears to the eyes of the audience. Before exiting the car to enter the clinic, her father turned to look at her and referring to her pregnancy said, "Honey, this is what you did, it is not who you are. God's grace is big enough to cover any mistake."

As she wiped her eyes, she shared how she had to break the news later to her husband. We all leaned forward in our seats waiting for her to tell us what his reaction was to her betrayal. She relayed to us just how blessed she was to have such a good Christian man in her life. Before her words were even out of her mouth, her husband walked down the center aisle carrying their sleeping two-year-old in his arms to stand beside her at the altar.

In an act of love and grace only God could have given him, she told the crowd he willingly adopted the child. A story of forgiveness that powerful cannot be listened to without tears.

We had seen firsthand God's grace unfold in the life of this couple. The sin, the repentance, the forgiveness, and finally the reconciliation inspired us. That moment was worth the price of the whole conference. It gave me renewed confidence that even in our most strained and broken relationships, we have hope.

As we gathered our conference notes and supplies together, we headed back to our last hotel for the final night. The day's events had taught me God's grace and forgiveness can't be crowded out by my concerns for the next day. Yet, as we prepared for the journey home, our faith was going to be tested again. Though my employer had deposited the requested funds, expenses had exceeded our careful calculations. Our remaining moneys would be insufficient to cover the required tax payment for the rental.

The return trip back to Sky Harbor airport filled me with dread. What would the rental agent do when we would say we couldn't pay for the remaining balance on the car when we returned it? With simple childlike trust, Le Anne laid her hand on my arm and said softly, "Let's pray about it before we go in." We reminded God that we had come out to Phoenix for His divine purpose of training families in reconciliation. We made known our circumstances and asked Him to please let the customer service desk have mercy on us since we were about $100 short. As we made our way slowly out of the car on our trek to the rental desk, my mouth was dry. My churning stomach only added to my anxiety.

I didn't know that God was going to school me again, that He has ways of answering prayer that I simply could never comprehend. As I approached the desk, I nervously placed the car keys on the counter and before I could even utter a word, the attendant apprised us, "I am so sorry, but this building is having electrical problems. All our computers are down, and we cannot transact any business." In fact, he remarked, "It's odd, our building is the only one experiencing the issue. If you are in a hurry to catch your flight, we'll call you when you arrive back home, and you can pay over the phone at that time." With a simple thank you for riding with us comment, he waved us on to our gate. Stunned at the Lord's miracle, He had already resolved our problem before we had even asked.

The call from the rental company did not come for a full week after we got home. By then, we had received our regular paycheck, and the bill had become a simple task. God's power that day and in the days ahead, would continue to humble and fill us with hope and awe.

"So do not fear, for I am with you, do not be dismayed, for I am your God.

I will strengthen you and help you; I will uphold you with my righteous right hand." Isaiah 41:10 (NIV)

God of the Flies

"Again, truly I tell you that if two of you on earth agree about anything they ask for, it will be done for them by my Father in heaven. For where two or three gather in my name, there am I with them." Matthew 18:19-20 (NIV)

Each Fall, my smallest country church planned a special outing. These events were designed to help first-time visitors feel comfortable with church in a non-church setting. The relaxed atmosphere allowed our members to invite friends and family to join us. When the autumn leaves would reach their peak of brilliance, the little congregation would assemble at a nearby state park for a day of outdoor church, singing, a picnic and a hike. It was always the highlight of the year.

The park straddles two state lines and boasts a five-mile gorge that plunges over 1,650 feet deep. It is affectionately known by the locals as "The Grand Canyon of the South." The park has scenic hiking trails, breathtaking river vistas, many picnic areas, and even a museum. Inside the museum, a genuine Kentucky moonshine still is on display. The still, and the plaque that explains its history, always intrigues me. While the spirit still moves in these mountains, this particular type of Kentucky spirit would have been at least 100 proof.

One year, as I stood reading the inscription, I felt an urgent tug on my sleeve. Expecting to find one of the churches children seeking my attention, I turned around to find a little doe instead. This adorable animal had a sweet disposition. I later learned that having been hit by a car, she was given sanctuary in the park in order to convalesce. The doe had become so used to the park visitors that she was no longer afraid. She would beg for carrots and her favorite food of apples. I found it a joy, that when I was preaching, she would wander into the picnic pavilion hoping for treats. Much to the children's delight, she would often follow along on the afternoon hike as well.

We had chosen this time of year for our outing because of the fine weather. The morning air was crisp, but by the afternoon it would be comfortably warm. This was beneficial as it lowered the risk of being pestered by mosquitoes and gnats. In prior years this strategy had worked well, so we had taken it for granted that it would work well again. However, as we worshiped that year, things were quite different. Small swarms of unwelcome insects began harassing us.

The mosquitoes ushered in the no-see-um gnats, the sweat bees and soon the flies followed. They seemed to have but one purpose – ruining our church gathering and picnic. As I preached in the open-air pavilion, I recognized the signs of a distracted audience. Each attendee had become so preoccupied with swatting our mini plague that no one was listening. I stopped midway through my sermonette and said, "Friends, God is Lord over everything—including these flies. Let's ask Him right now to drive these pests away so we can enjoy our time together." I knew firsthand that I could pray in confidence, because in times of my own doubt, God had shown His love in ways that always astounded me.

What I didn't know was this was about to became a transformational teaching moment for one of my senior members. Unbeknownst to me was a situation with the church member's granddaughter who had burdened her grandmother that week by sharing struggles that were becoming overwhelming. The granddaughter felt that God wasn't listening to her and thus didn't care. As I made the statement that we should bow our heads, and ask God to drive away the insects, the grandmother was harboring doubt that God would hear my simple request.

While I prayed for God's involvement, she wrestled with the thought…wasn't a swarm of miserable insects *unimportant* to God? In a moment, she had her answer. As I said, "Amen," the cloud of irritating bugs immediately began to dissipate. Within five minutes, the area had become free of all annoyances. God had not only answered my request, he had done so in record time.

The remainder of our day was filled with praise, good food, laughter, and continued appearances by the much-anticipated friendly doe. We had found favor with God during our little gathering. Often when misfortune occurs, we hear it described as an "Act of God." But, when life does go well, it is sad that God seldom gets the credit He so richly deserves.

Some weeks later, I received an unexpected note from my senior member. She praised the Lord for the miracle of the disappearing insects. Because of that incident, her faith had increased exponentially. Upon returning to her home following the days outing, she had written an encouraging letter to her granddaughter. Her message: "If God can hear and answer a little prayer about insects, I am most confident He can handle any struggles going on in your life."

I find it comforting that I personally know some of the many names of Jesus. I have needed every one of them in my life. Jesus is known as The Comforter, Our Advocate, The Prince of Peace, and by hundreds more names that hold special meanings for each of us. That day at the park, I added another name to His impressive list: God of the Flies. His love and power never cease to amaze me! Praise His name!

It Lit the Evening Sky

"The LORD will keep you from all harm— he will watch over your life; the Lord will watch over your coming and going both now and forevermore." Psalm 121: 7,8 (NIV)

It was a rare day when I was home; today was one of them. Relaxing in the living room, I was jolted upright by our daughter Toni's scream. I don't know how God does it, but He gives parents added wisdom in knowing what kind of scream deems immediate attention and which ones are just playful. This one needed immediate attention. As I ran to the rear of the house where our daughter's room was, I smelled something electrically hot. She quickly told me she was simply unplugging the lamp next to her bed, when a long flame shot out and left a black oval burn mark on her bedroom wall. Fortunately, the pie plate size spot was easily cleaned up but the issues with the house were beginning to become more frequent.

During our interminable long wait for compensation, it seemed like we were always trying to make do. When it came to plumbing or electric, the home had a plethora of surprises. One day we smelled something hot and found our window air conditioning unit plug had melted into the wall outlet. Another time, our brand-new pool pump burned out. Even the central heat and air unit for the house fried its circuit board and rendered us dependent on a fireplace insert for a better part of a year. It was always something.

To remedy our heating needs, a friend graciously gave us a large fireplace insert. The cast iron stove felt like it weighed a ton. It took five of us to carry it in and set it on the hearth. But, prior to inserting it into the opening, we wisely inspected the interior of the flue and learned the brick interior of the chimney had wide gaps between the mortar. Since the house had multiple fractured floor joists, apparently the chimney was not immune from the settling either.

I recall one day while entertaining guests, I heard a loud odd snapping noise. It sounded like someone had taken a chair and slammed it down twice full force onto our hardwood floors. The sound caught us off guard. With the added weight of our guests, the floor joists below our table were splintering in real-time. We had to stop using our dining room from that point on. The hardwood flooring was the only thing that kept the subflooring from caving into the home's crawlspace. We were warned it was best to eat in a front room until future repairs could be made.

With everyone waiting on me to go to the hardware store for heat caulking, I returned as fast as I could with a case of twelve heat resistant tubes of caulk to complete the job. The interior of the chimney was really bad; we needed every one of those tubes. My friend being the handy type, assembled a riveted metal liner box that went into the top of the chimney like a straw descending into a beverage. We were most cautious as we inserted the long square tube, to avoid the power line above the house. He had measured it correctly and it slid into place with only a couple of taps with a rubber mallet. The new chimney flue offered us an additional layer of protection against fire, in case more bricks separated within the tall stack.

The jobs both complete, we finally slid the heavy beast into place within the hearth. The stove became a significant blessing. In the winter it kept the main parts of the house in the low 80's and the ends of the house where our bedrooms were, in the upper 60's.

On the coldest days, we would stock the firebox full and close the damper and the slower burn would keep the house warm in our absence. The drawback to turning the damper tighter was it could allow creosote to build up inside the chimney. We tried our best to burn only the driest wood but sometimes we weren't diligent enough. The black tar (creosote) heightened the likelihood of a chimney fire if the chimney was not frequently cleaned. We had it cleaned twice in concurrent years, so we didn't give much thought, as we drove off to one of our churches eighty-four miles away.

Because of the great distances between our churches, it was not uncommon for us to be gone all day and return home late into the evening. This cold night my wife went into the house to start the fire. Jesse and I decided to grab a few armloads of wood before we came into the house. As my wife opened the door to the stove, she thought it odd to hear a mighty rush of air followed by a rumble. She didn't see what we were seeing. But what she couldn't see was impressive. Like a meteor lighting a darkened sky, our whole back yard and mountainside lit up like it was daylight. For a minute I remember thinking, "why is it so bright out here at eleven o'clock at night? It was then he yelled, "Dad, there's a chimney fire!"

As I gazed upward, it was majestic, in an eerie sort of way. It had the appearance of the methane flames we'd see burning on smokestacks at local oil and gas refineries. However, this flame wasn't on a factory, it was on our house! We immediately sprang into action. My wife shut down the stove damper to cut off the fire's oxygen while Jesse ran into the house and came out with a gallon pitcher of water. He scrambled up over porch roof onto the main house roof, like a spider monkey and threw the container of water down the chimney opening. It didn't appear to make much difference, so he rushed back down and inside for another round. The second dousing worked.

As quickly as it started, it was over. Despite the adrenaline rush, I told my wife before her head hit the pillow, "Good news, the chimney's as clean as a whistle now!" I always boasted I married my wife for her looks, but they surely weren't the ones she was giving me tonight.

It was a few months later when our second event occurred. This time, by way of our next-door neighbor. It was near midnight on a Tuesday night and we were again just walking in the door from driving the long distance back from prayer meeting. Tired, we were taking our jackets off when without warning, a large boom shook our home. Our daughter being the fastest in the family, ran towards the sound at the opposite end of the house and breathlessly yelled back to us, "Dad, there's a fire outside!"

We rushed to look out her bedroom window and saw the bright glow four-hundred feet away at the end of our property, illuminating the midnight sky. Putting our jackets back on, my children were as eager as me for another adventure. My wife on the other hand, was non-plussed, "I'm going to bed," she stated flatly. For her, our life was enough of a rollercoaster, one more loop in the track today was not necessary. She was exhausted and not interested at all in taking part. On the other hand, I found life adventuresome even if it was at my own expense. Having originally been a newscaster when I was in college, I had never lost my desire to get the "scoop" on a juicy news story. Our children had inherited the same gene.

As the three of us hopped in the family car and drove the short distance to our neighbor's yard, the home had the appearance of a glowing coal furnace. From stem to stern, it was completely engulfed in flames. As we pulled into the driveway and just before jumping out of the car, the sounds of incendiary devices (most likely propane tanks and bullets), were exploding. We quickly backed the car out of the driveway to watch from a safer distance. Fortunately, no one was home. I was shocked that despite the intensity of the fire and explosions, not one person in our neighboring holler elicited any interest at all. Apparently, it must have been a fairly common occurrence.

As I dialed 911, and apprised the operator of the inferno, she asked me if they needed to send an ambulance. Watching the ferocity of the flames, I told her that if the owner was inside, the only thing they would need to send would be a dustpan and a broom.

We waited twenty minutes for the volunteer fire department and police to arrive, but oddly law enforcement never showed up. Apparently, they shared the same attitude as the neighbors: apathy. It took the firemen a while to douse the hinges because that's about all that was left of the house. Later, we learned from another neighbor, this was the fourth house fire this same family had had in fourteen years. Tired, we returned the short distance home and flopped into bed. Another adventure had been tucked away and added to our memory banks.

Throughout our time in Appalachia, we shared our unbelievable stories with community churches in our town. Often the remarks of the congregants would be something like, "You seem like the bible character Job." I would always laugh and reply, "No, far from it. If you remember at the end of Job's trials

God blessed him and his wife with ten more children. If that would happen to us, you can be sure this story would have a more exciting conclusion. My wife would kill me."

When God Calls, Please Answer

"And the God of all grace, who called you to His eternal glory in Christ, after you have suffered a little while, will Himself restore you and make you strong, firm and steadfast." I Peter 5:10 (NIV)

What's not to love about Florida in the winter? We had been attending winter meetings there and what a pleasant change it was from the cold air at home. The week had rewarded the family with warm ocean breezes during the day and rhythmic waves lulling us to sleep at night. What a difference from the blustery winds and frigid temperatures back home. If there was an opportunity to travel anywhere, we jumped at it. Who turns down indoor plumbing in winter when they have been using an outdoor porta-a-john that feels like a frozen meat locker? It was so refreshing being "normal," even if only for a week.

As the conference was coming to an end, we began dreading the long eleven-hour drive home. We would have preferred to have started a day earlier, only because we had evangelism meetings beginning the next night. Sadly we had no choice. We lacked the extra funds to pay for a hotel stay on the way home. Our tight budget for travel and food had been exhausted and it would be a long month before we would be reimbursed. Whatever the challenges–house, lawsuit, or vehicles–life always seemed to outstrip the paycheck long before the month was over.

If the journey home had a musical genre, the theme would have been the blues. It was depressing leaving a state we loved, where we had so many wonderful memories. The further we drove, the more the scenery deteriorated. It was as if nature was feeling as morose as we were. The tree lines descended from beautiful hues of green to unadorned brown coatracks.

In my head, I envisioned us as morning radio personalities for a failing radio station. We would cheerfully laugh and encourage others. For our churches' sake, we had to keep everybody else's spirits positive, but what about ours? Each time we would return home, the only thing we could count on being normal was the setting on the clothes dryer. No one truly knew the crushing weight of living in the constant chaos that regularly surrounded us.

As we topped the mountains coming back into Kentucky, it was often the time my prayer warrior wife Le Anne would pray the hardest. Several years later she confessed to me that each time we crested those ridges, anxiety would crop up, her pulse would race, and her chest would tighten. She has always been my rock but no more so than in the ministry we shared. I am confident that had I married anyone else, countless other women would have bolted and left me long behind. What made her special was she knew God's hand and heart and she stayed faithful to us both.

We arrived back home both famished and with a fuel tank nearing empty. Time was short. We barely had time to unload the car, make a quick peanut butter sandwich, and change into a fresh set of clothes before we headed out to the evangelism series. The children, glad to be home, chose to stay put. They were happy to escape the confines of our cramped car and one more meeting. As we were about to leave the house, we faced yet another dilemma. How would we drive one-hundred twenty miles round trip on an eighth of a tank of gas? We knew God needed us at the meetings but how would we get there with no money and no fuel?

Then a thought popped into Le Anne's head: why not retrieve an old garden hose from the garage. Moments later, she returned with the long green tube while I set to opening our old bus's steel gas cap. Once opened, she placed one end of the hose in the tank and passed me the other end. "You've got more hot air then I've got, so get to sucking!" Within moments, I resembled a withered apple face doll. As I sucked away with abandon on the offending hose, my hollowed cheeks became as red as an embarrassed lobster.

The fuel seemed to take forever to course its way through the medium length hose, but my wife was correct, I did have more air than her–a whole lot of air. I tried to listen for the approaching liquid, but it surprised me. In fact, it caught me off guard. I was revulsed as a mouthful of eighty-seven octane liberally washed my tonsils. I can tell you from experience, that once gas enters your mouth, you'll be tasting and burping it for the better part of a day. Understanding the flammable nature of gasoline, I felt the need to be overly cautious. I wanted to avoid anyone smoking nearby less the fumes combusted spontaneously and caused me to become the defacto president of the Ignited Way.

As distasteful as it was, I was optimistic this would only be a one-time thing. Surely the Lord would provide the means necessary to make our meetings. I mean, they were really His meetings, weren't they? I can attest that He indeed kept His word. He provided all the fuel we needed as I siphoned gas every day for a week. I knew the bus's gas tank didn't have a lot in its reservoir, but the miracle of providing all the fuel I needed to drive the one-hundred twenty miles round-trip each day never faltered.

Eight days had passed since the meetings had begun and I had finished preaching at one of my three churches that Saturday morning. As was my custom, I stood at the front door after the service shaking hands with everyone as they left. Out of the corner of my eye, I noticed one of the older members waiting to speak with me. She shifted awkwardly from one foot to the other as she waited for everyone to leave. After everyone was gone, she sheepishly approached me.

As I greeted her by name, I glanced down at the tightly held, white envelope in her hands. It wasn't my birthday and it wasn't pastor appreciation, so I was confused as to what was in it. Hanging her head, she softly made a halting confession.

"Pastor, since last week, the Holy Spirit has been telling me you needed this and I refused to listen. I kept putting it off, but as the week progressed, He became more forceful and now this is weighing heavy on my heart. I believe you truly need this. So here, I want you to have this!"

Shoving the envelope into my hands, she mumbled a quick goodbye and hurried out the front door. I was curious to its contents. As I reached inside the envelope, I was astonished. It contained sixty dollars! Three crisp twenty-dollar bills peaked out of the envelope. It was just the amount of funds I would need to purchase gas for the remainder of the meetings.

It was a valuable lesson for the giver and for me. She had not listened to the Holy Spirit's prompting, and I had been inconvenienced and discouraged for an entire week. It served as a reminder to me that when the Lord calls, answer Him immediately. My heart sang with the realization that my days of sucking and tasting gas were over. It also prompted a stirring in me. If the Spirit needed me to do anything–give someone a call, write a letter, or meet a need–I wanted to be faithful, and respond quickly. I never want anyone to hurt or to go without simply because I failed to do what God had prompted me to do.

The meetings ended with not one soul deciding for Christ, but the lesson learned was success is not as important as being faithful. I attended every night and God was honored; I did everything He had asked of me. Lord, let me have faith in your provision and fill my heart every day from a tank like my old bus, never ending.

The Appalachian Rock Salt Miracle

"The LORD is my rock, my fortress and my deliverer; my God is my rock, in whom I take refuge..." Psalm 18:2 (NIV)

If it's a bargain, I'm going to buy it, even if I don't need it. It was early Spring, and I was walking out of a Dollar General in town. That's when I saw it, sitting all by itself on the shelf. It was a large plastic container of rock salt. I wrestled with whether I needed it since the season was almost over. Yet, the price was too good to pass up. "Maybe it will come in handy," I thought as I placed it in my cart. I'm always proud of a good "find", and this particular deal was 70% off.

I paid for my other desired items and promptly placed the large plastic jug in the trunk of my car. My wife hates clutter, so my trunk always has something that seems to be rolling roll around in it. So, I thought maybe today I would appease her with my bargain hunting prowess. "Who knows", I mused, "We may need it sometime." Despite my wife's request to store the rock salt in the garage, I fought the urge to do her bidding and left it in the trunk. I was glad that, for this time at least, I had ignored her pleas. Though only there for about a week, the miracle as to why soon became crystal clear.

Overseeing three churches miles apart meant we had a lot of road to cover. We had just finished the morning service at one church and, now in the car, were eating sandwiches as we drove to the afternoon service sixty-five miles away. The ride that day was beautiful. The snow had begun to melt, and hints of Spring were in the air. Some of the trees had started to bud and it was always a welcome sight to gaze on the familiar Dogwood and Red Bud trees. Earlier in the morning the roads had been covered in a thin layer of black ice but, thankfully by afternoon, the sun had warmed most of them and it was smooth sailing...until now.

Traveling this frequent mountain road, we came to a curve where it had been carved out between two rock ledges. The sides were tall, and the sun hadn't had a chance to remain on the road long enough to cast its warmth. As the sun moved past, shadows began to appear, and refreezing of the road began. It had created a surface as slick as petroleum jelly. Driving at 60 miles per hour we entered the curved canyon. As we rounded the bend, without warning, we met certain disaster.

Ahead of us, another car had met the same icy patch but with dreadful results. Why the police had not stationed anyone at the beginning of the curve was beyond me. A mere 100 yards ahead of us, an ambulance crew was loading up victims of a car wreck. As I stepped on my brakes, my heart leaped into my throat; the ice had made my brakes useless.

I'm told its customary, when you face a life, or death situation, a myriad number of processes will run through your mind. I could have thought of my short life and how close I was to buying the farm. I could have had thoughts of innocent lives being wiped out in the ambulance or that my family was facing certain death. But, oddly, that's not what went through my mind. I'm embarrassed to say that my first thought was, "Mother of Pearl! My insurance rates are now going to skyrocket!" Setting that selfish thought aside, I had a split second to make up my mind what I was going to do.

Seeing the panic in the eyes of the ambulance crew as I careened towards them, I had a choice: I could hit them and their occupants or turn sharply down a snow-covered embankment, risk going off a ledge and land on top of the roof of a manufactured house below. I chose to take my chances with the embankment and advised everyone in the car to hang on. As the car lurched down the sloping hill, we traveled about 50 feet before we stopped suddenly in the snow. The prevailing thought was it was either deeper than we thought, or our angel had stopped us, before we jettisoned off the ledge.

With the sudden stop, it was then I remembered my bargain container of rock salt. With no chance to calm my shaky legs, I jumped out of the car, popped the trunk, and ran back up the hill to the road. Quickly, with a wide sweeping motion of my arm, I began spreading the rock salt from the container as fast as I could. It was none too soon. For just as I had finished dumping its contents, coming around the corner was a tractor trailer at a high rate of speed–just like I had done moments before. He too saw the entire scene and slammed on his brakes. I held my breath as he started to skid toward the ambulance and mangled car. That is, until he came to the patch of rock salt. His tires catching the salt, he came to a stop a mere 50 yards from broadsiding the ambulance and its occupants. My jug of salt had averted two major catastrophes, in a matter of minutes!!!

We missed church that afternoon, but it didn't matter. I received my blessing for the day and then some. God revealed His loving care to me in the most dramatic of ways. He became both my Rock, and Rock Salt, of my salvation. That plastic container sure was more than a bargain!

The Appointed Anointed Detour

> "And we know that in all things God works for the good of those who love him, who have been called according to his purpose." Romans 8:28 (NIV)

Since we drove such an exorbitant number of miles annually, I was always on the lookout for inexpensive vehicles as a backup option. I had purchased an older model white Cadillac from a nice church member. The price had been right, and the smooth ride was pure luxury. The burgundy tufted seats were similar to the interior of a high-end casket, but I didn't care; oh, how I loved that car. It was long and sleek, had fins at the back, over its tail lights. It was a dependable car and gave us good service for a year. It could pass anything, except a gas station. Despite its age, it was in almost perfect condition, except for a crack in the left rear fin.

One weekend, we drove it to church and decided to leave it in the parking lot overnight. We had a church work project planned for the next morning, and it seemed the engine's water pump might be failing. So, leaving it there, we spent the night with friends.

When we returned the next morning, it became clear that we had made a bad decision. Our only car now looked like it had been the lead vehicle in a military battle. The front windshield was a spider web of cracks. Thirteen BB gun pellets had damaged the glass beyond repair. The driver's side window had been smashed in–probably with a baseball bat. Broken glass covered the seats and interior of the car like confetti. The glove compartment had been ransacked and its papers were strewn throughout the car and parking lot. It appeared that the neighborhood children had enjoyed the "fun" of vandalism. With all the damage, it became evident that we would need a new car; the window replacements alone would exceed than the value of the vehicle.

Over the years, my wife had learned a lot from our many trials. She was quick to remind me that whenever hardships and misfortunes occurred, we should consider them to be God's anointed detours. If plans were delayed, it would be because God had purposes behind the setbacks. The thought of this eased my mind and took the distress out of our situation. From her wisdom, my perspective changed from viewing it as adversity, to seeing it, as an opportunity.

My uncle owned a car sales business in Florida. Perhaps he could find another vehicle for us at a reasonable price. Short-notice plane tickets were far too expensive for our meager finances, so I chose to ride the bus to Florida. Because we were eighty-seven miles from home, and the buses didn't run to that area, I had to leave from that location.

With no luggage or spare clothes, I set out on my unplanned adventure. As the family was being driven back home by friends, I was on what would be the longest and most grueling bus ride of my life. Recognizing that this trip had to be an "appointed detour," I asked God to give me patience, and to help me see the situation with fresh eyes.

My first seatmate was a tall college basketball player, who had been flirting with the idea of going professional. Returning home to attend a funeral, he was unsure about what he was going to tell his family. He shared with me his misgivings and fears about being a professional player, and what stardom would mean for his life. His desire was for a simple way of living, and he felt that God was urging him to do something more meaningful. He knew the pitfalls of that fast-paced life, and he'd seen how it had adversely affected his teammates. It was his family's dream for him to "make it big." Now, he was hesitant to share his doubts with them.

One of the things we discussed was the advice written in Matthew 6:33. That text says our priority must be to seek first the kingdom of God and His righteousness, and then everything else will be added to us (paraphrased). He was quiet as he thought about what I had said. We both knew that our encounter had to have been providential, because he mentioned the timeliness of my council. Before he stepped off the bus, we had a prayer that God's plan for his life would become clear. He also prayed that God would give him the needed confidence to tell his parents what was truly in his heart: that he didn't want his life's journey to be all about basketball.

A few stops later we picked up a woman passenger in North Carolina. Work was not easy to find in her hometown, so she was travelling to a disaster area to start a new job with the federal agency, FEMA. As we sat together, she revealed that she was a single mom with several children. It was causing her anxiety having to leave her children behind with friends.

I shared with her that God has promised us peace, no matter the situation. I paraphrased 1 John 4:18 for her and explained that God's perfect love casts out our fear. I suggested that it may be His plan for her, that she should have this time to be alone with Him. As the miles slipped away, she began to take comfort from that thought. Before she disembarked at her stop, she expressed to me that our meeting must have been by God's design.

I had travelled almost eighteen hours without sleep and was quite tired. However, my weariness soon disappeared when I found myself sitting with another appointed traveler. This young man, like me, was also heading to Florida. He told me that he was travelling home for a family gathering. A Haitian by birth, he had been bereft of his parents but had been brought up by a loving Christian family. Our conversation took on more meaning when he asked what I did for work. I told him I was a pastor.

He followed up with, "What denomination are you?"

"I'm Seventh-day Adventist."

His eyes widened and he exclaimed, "I was brought up Seventh-day Adventist!" He began to tell me excitedly about his childhood, and what the church had meant to him.

I asked him if he still had a strong faith in God.

He hung his head. "No, I've gotten away from Him, and I've only recently been thinking about renewing my relationship with Him."

I posed another question, "Do you know that God is like a GPS? It doesn't matter where we deviate from our path in life, He will always recalculate where we are so we can find our way back to Him."

He smiled and listened carefully to my impromptu lesson. I shared with him how important he was to God. Soon after that, the bus driver announced arrival at our destination.

Before stepping off the bus, I turned back to him and said, "Do you really think this encounter was by chance? God wanted us to meet, so you could be reminded that it's never too late to come home." I gave him contact information for a church in the town where he was headed, and he promised me that he would attend.

I reached my journey's end feeling exhausted, but purposeful. I had done what God had directed me to do and He blessed me accordingly. My uncle in Tampa gave me a "sweet deal" on a luxurious late model Mercury Grand Marquis. That car would turn out to be my most favorite. God was blessing me with a vehicle that would exceed 300,000 miles of use, without any major mechanical problems.

Back home in Kentucky, I felt a renewed sense of happiness and purpose. The next week, we drove to church in our new car. The only thing that put a slight damper on my day was that I had forgotten to bring a jacket for the ride home in our beaten-up Cadillac. It was still sitting pathetically in the church parking lot. Jesse and I would drive it home, and Le Anne and Toni would drive the new Mercury.

The fall air was fresh and exhilarating, but as we drove 60 mph in a car with holes in the windshield and no driver's side window, it became uncomfortably frosty. To say it was "breezy" was an understatement. It felt like we were pilots in an open cockpit biplane. It was impossible to have a conversation over the sound of the whistling air passing through the BB-gun holes in the windshield. I became convinced that multiple boiling teakettles could not have made any more screeching noise than that. At least, with that ongoing loudness, we knew we wouldn't hit any deer on the way home – they would hear us coming!

When we reached home, we were both frozen and deafened from the journey. We covered our battered Cadillac with a tarp to keep out the rain, and then went inside to file an insurance claim. During the weeks of waiting for repairs, I had learned that one of my church members was in desperate need of a car. Thinking this was a cue from God to gift the car, I promised my friend that after the repairs were completed, he could have it.

A week later, a mobile repair van pulled up our steep driveway to begin the glass restoration process. As the two men removed the tarp from the Cadillac and opened the front door of the car, I heard a loud yell. I hurried outside to see what had caused all the commotion.

Unnerved, the men said that while the car had been sheltered, red wasps had built nests in both the door frame and the broken left fin. The day had warmed sufficiently so that the wasps were active and ready to fight. I gave the men a can of wasp spray, and soon the battle ended.

The copay on the insurance claim had left me with a sizeable out-of-pocket expense, yet I was happy to tell my church member that his car was ready. He was excited and couldn't wait to come to our house and slide behind the wheel of his "new" vehicle.

As he sat down in the driver's seat, this 4 foot 8-inch senior citizen disappeared behind the dashboard. He was so short that it seemed he would need phonebooks to sit on – just to see over the steering wheel. He was thrilled with his gift and was determined to drive it home. Later, his wife told me how she would find him just sitting in the plush seats of his car for hours, smiling over his good fortune.

As he descended our driveway and waved goodbye, I began laughing heartily. I realized that I had forgotten to tell him about the car's unique "security system"–it was now activated.

Due to the vibration of the car, the remaining wasps were now streaming out the rear fin, like a long black rope. For his sake, I prayed that the pests would be long gone, before he arrived home. I didn't want to be remembered, as the pastor who gave a gift that really stung.

My Gifts Were All the Buzz

"And do not forget to do good and to share with others, for with such sacrifices God is pleased."
Hebrews 13:16

Winter was fast approaching, and now that we had a fireplace insert, our old coal stove was no longer necessary. Our home sat in front of a 10-inch seam of coal that ran through our back hillside. When our house became too cold, we would simply grab a bucket and go outside to pick up chunks of coal that had sloughed off the mountain. Some of the pieces were so large that we had to break them up before throwing them into the stove.

The stove was finicky, and sometimes it was hard to get started. We found that using the thin tissue wrappers from the porta-potty rolls would provide kindling material for a quick start. We had a habit of tossing the paper inside it throughout the seasons. Once the stove would get going, its intense heat would get hot enough to melt the crown molding on the ceiling above it – and one time it did.

One day, I received a call from a church member who had an odd problem. He was the recipient of a six-ton pile of coal but didn't have the money to buy a coal stove. The type of stove we had, and no longer needed, was tall and narrow. It would be the perfect fit for his singlewide mobile home. We offered it to him for free, with the caveat that he would have to pick it up and haul it away.

The following Sunday, after shoveling his last pile of coal, and driving it home in his pickup, he came to our house. When he arrived, I showed him our coal stove, extolled its virtues, and demonstrated how to operate it. As we got ready to disassemble it, I opened the top to peer inside. Quickly, I slammed the lid back down.

Seeing my look of disbelief, he asked, "What?"

"You're not going to believe this. I hope you can wait about thirty minutes before we take this apart."

He agreed but inquired as to why the wait.

"Because, inside this stove are more red wasps than I have ever seen gathered into one place. The stove is absolutely full of them!"

The day was cold, and I was glad for that as it resulted in the wasps being somewhat lethargic. I knew all too well how agonizing a wasp sting could be. I was reminded of a previous winter evening. Snow was on the ground, and I was cozied up in bed reading the newspaper, when I felt what I thought was a strong electrical shock to my shoulder. I immediately grabbed the painful spot then felt a second surprising jolt to my jaw. I threw down the newspaper and jumped up yelling. As I looked around, I saw the detestable winged insect flying toward the ceiling fan like it was intoxicated. The red wasp had fallen from the ceiling and stung me twice – in mid-January.

My wife and younger son had come running to see what the noise was all about. Jesse rolled up the newspaper and stood on the bed, ready to enact retaliation.

"No, wait!" I pointed toward the closet. "Get the vacuum cleaner!"

"Why, Dad?"

"Because it's bagless, and when you suck him up, he will die a slow death while looking out at the world from his lonely prison window!"

I didn't have to wait long for my vengeance, for soon he was sucked into oblivion. His act of terrorism was forgotten only after the swelling on my jaw went down.

Now, as I stood in front of the coal stove with my church member at my side, we contemplated our next move. I flicked a lit match into the stove and quickly slammed the door. Within seconds the wastepaper inside burst into flame, and a rushing noise was heard inside the stovepipe. Woosh! Several generations of wasp families met their burning Sodom-and-Gomorrah-like end. I was triumphant! My revenge had been served *hot*. I went outside to look at what was coming out of the pipe. It appeared, from all the white smoke on our side of the mountain, that a new pope had just been elected.

It took thirty minutes before the stove and its pipe were cool enough before we could load it onto our friend's truck. I saw him a few weeks later and he told me the stove worked fabulously. When he installed it, he had run the pipe out of a window, attached it with straps away from the eaves, and was enjoying free heat for the winter.

One of the drawbacks of burning coal is that it generates a lot of dust. The black dust clings to the interior of a pipe and can restrict its airflow. Occasionally, the pipe requires a tap on the exterior to clear and settle the dust. My friend told me that one time he had returned home from a day's hard work. His wife had just finished cleaning in preparation for the Sabbath, and she was proud of her spotless house. Their house was getting chilly, so he attempted to start the coal stove, but found that the draft was restricted.

As he had done many times before, he took the end of a broom handle and tapped on the pipe. A gentle tap had always cleared the metal stovepipe, but without thinking, this time he hit it far too hard. It separated and fell apart. Time seemed to stand still as both he and his wife stood by helplessly and watched a rolling cloud of choking coal dust settle over the interior of the house. He never did tell me his wife's response – he didn't have to. Knowing his wife, I'm confident he became an expert at coal dust removal.

Not every gift is a welcome blessing; some are meant to teach us a lesson, such as patience. My family and I also received a benefit, in that after sharing our stove, we saw nary a red wasp for two years. The Good Book is correct. It *is* more blessed to give then to receive.

Fire on the Mountain

"When you pass through the waters, I will be with you, and through the rivers, they will not sweep over you or overwhelm you. When you walk through the fire, you will not be burned or scorched, nor the flames set you ablaze." Isaiah 43:2 (NIV)

For eight years we'd been living in our house. It had been rare for my wife and I to be apart. Our unpredictable home had been a source of alarm and annoyance. It was like leaving little children with a teenage babysitter, and for the same reason: what will the condition of the house be, when we return? Now with our own cherubs off to Christian boarding school and college, I hated to leave my wife alone. It was an urgent family matter that required me to be gone for three days.

While we were apart the first two days, the conversation was light banter, but the third day, all that changed. As I was readying myself to board my flight home, my cellphone rang. On the other end my wife's breathless voice was urgent. "JOHN, THE BARN AND GARAGE IS GONE! I'm not sure I can save the house. I've called the fire department they're on their way, the flames are on all three sides of the house. I'm pulling things out of the house now, COME HOME SOON, I'VE GOT TO GO!" There was a click and the phone went dead.

I froze. A million thoughts began running through my mind as I envisioned the scenario before her. What caused *this* new crisis? What blew up, combusted, or worked loose? How did this happen? (We later learned someone had thrown a lit cigarette out their car window into the dry leaves and kept driving.) My wife only learned there was a fire when she smelled smoke in the house; our huge garage had obscured the view of the flames at the back of the property. Running outside, she swung open the garage's twelve-foot doors and found the back-half totally engulfed in flames. Gas cans and camping propane tanks sat mere inches from the flames. She bravely tried to pull on the new Teardrop camper we had just purchased but something was wedged under the wheel. With but seconds to spare before the gas and propane ignited, she wisely slammed the doors. With her heart pounding, she ran back across the driveway and inside the house to call 911.

Amazingly, not one neighbor or passing car called the fire department to report the flames. The fire had been raging for some time and it was exacting. Like a force field, it had oddly consumed only the six and half acres of *our* property on the side of a mountain. As if the Devil was taunting us, the flames stopped precisely at each of our neighbor's property lines.

I could only imagine the fear Le Anne was facing at that very moment. The number of near misses and tragedies our house had experienced over the years were too many to mention! We often chided each other that we weren't in need of a carpenter as much as we needed an exorcist. Multiple times we were spared the loss of our house to some quirky happenstance, only because the Lord spared us from each loss.

Though the situation sounded dire, I knew one source of strength and peace I could call on was God. I had difficulty forming my words, as I envisioned the fire. How did this happen? Is Le Anne safe? Would the house even be standing, when I got back? As I took my seat on the plane, I would be having an uninterrupted conversation with God. The urgent updates would have to wait; I would be inaccessible by phone for the two-hour flight back home.

As I ruminated on this new episode, I was angry. How was it that we were so busy for the Lord and yet, we couldn't seem to catch our breath from one crisis to another? I was so sick of this house and all its problems; I was grateful in some ways I wasn't there. Because, unlike my wife trying to save the family heirlooms inside, I would have been outside with a bellows the size of a Volkswagen, fanning the flames for God, to finally get rid of it. After eight years of mindless litigation, broken pipes, electrical problems and the outhouse, I was done!

When the plane touched down, I immediately placed a call home. The house had been spared, but everything in the garage including our camping equipment, my beloved grandfather's camping stove, my tools, the children's bikes and yard implements were all gone. As I drove up the driveway into the smoky yard, my wife ran to meet me in tears and collapsed in my arms. She had experienced her own hell and if it weren't for God answering her prayers of desperation, the house and possibly her life would have been lost.

With a shaky voice, she recounted how the flames had jumped the driveway from the garage and barn, then raced up the hillside behind the house to consume our piece of the mountain. Then, for some unknown reason, the fire suddenly turned south on the property line and began burning back down towards the house, inexplicably stopping four-hundred feet away from the back bedrooms. She, painfully relived how she quickly began the task of removing family heirlooms from the house: a cedar chest, picture albums, and few books from my desk. The only place not burning was the front lawn, so she drug the items there. As red-hot flying embers kept igniting the pine needles and mulch around the foundation of the house, she dutifully kept dousing them with water from the garden hose, alternatingly spraying the roof should a stray spark start a new blaze. An escape route was ever in her mind, in case, the flames reversed their course and ignited the small front yard of the house.

She recounted how she had rushed in and out of the house numerous times, dutifully keeping watch on the smoldering mulch. As she had stood spraying the water, she was praying out loud reminding God that this was all we had and to please save it. At the height of being overwhelmed, a most welcome sound was heard–the sound of approaching sirens. Our friend and captain of the volunteer fire department had finally arrived with his crew, pulled into the driveway, and began battling the flames. Being a minister himself, he was a compassionate man and knowing I was absent, stayed with my wife, until I arrived home.

It's jarring to come back to a place devastated by fire. The skeletal remains of our once gigantic garage and majestic tree lay in charred rubble, still smoldering. The air conditioner had to be turned off; the heaviness of the smoke was overwhelming and was being sucked back into the house. The acrid smell and light haze would continue to hang over the property for weeks. As we went through the motions of trying to settle in for the night, Le Anne noticed something peculiar. Leaning down, she took a sniff of her arm and then the t-shirt she had worn throughout the fiery day. She suddenly realized something miraculous.

Holding out her arm and then the bottom of her shirt, she beckoned me with a command, "Smell this."

Leaning over I stated, "I don't smell anything," my voice trailing off in an inquisitive way.

"Exactly!" she exclaimed excitedly. With widening eyes, she continued "I have been wearing this shirt all day. It should smell like smoke, but it doesn't! And neither does my skin! It's just like the story in the Bible of the three Hebrew boys in the fiery furnace; their clothes didn't smell like smoke either! God had protected them in the fire, and He protected me, too!" Recognizing she had just experienced a true miracle, we both choked back tears of gratitude.

After a restless sleep, the following morning we surveyed the damage. Until now, we were unaware of the collateral damage the fire had enacted. There had been a powerline running from the garage, over the driveway, and connecting to the house. As it fell off the burning building, it landed in water from the fire hoses. The ensuing result was every third outlet in the house had shorted out and become inoperable. For several weeks afterwards, the interior of our house resembled a worksite, a spiderweb of yellow extension cords running in and out of various rooms. The refrigerator had to be plugged into an outlet in the living room, lamps in the living room had to be connected to the hallway outlets, and the microwave was now residing in my office.

Beside the desperate need of an electrician, our most urgent concern centered on a planned trip to Washington State for a job interview. My wife was reticent to leave the house but, for me, the trip was fortuitous. With all the problems, there was nothing to do here. At least we could relax a little and spend some much-needed time with friends. Besides, there would be no risk at night of spraining an ankle on an extension cord while fumbling one's way to the outhouse (at least for a week).

As we drove to the airport to catch our flight, Le Anne again expressed her misgivings about taking this trip. It was simply coming at the wrong time. I laughed out loud. If we stayed home every time something went wrong, we'd never leave the driveway. She chided, remember Murphy's Law, where everything that can go wrong, will go wrong? We were properly convinced we now resided in Murphy's own house! I remember vividly saying, as we drove away, "Honey relax, what more could possibly go wrong, while we're away? Four days later, we had the answer to that question.

Slip Sliding Away

> "The righteous cry out, and the LORD hears them; He delivers them from all their troubles. The LORD is close to the brokenhearted and saves those who are crushed in spirit. The righteous person may have many troubles, but the LORD delivers him from them all." Psalm 34:17-19 (NIV)

Our four days in Washington State had been just "what the doctor ordered." We forgot our troubles back home, and at least for a short period of time, life took on some normalcy. The views of Mt. Rainier were majestic, and the pungent smell of the tall pine trees was glorious.

Our companions and close friends were consummate hosts, taking us to numerous famous places. We visited Pike's Place Fish Market, the seafood store known for the tradition of fish-throwing as they serve their customers. We were shown beautiful lakes and numerous lush green forests. Another was an out-of-the-way quaint little restaurant at the base of the mountain. Known mostly to the locals, their specialty was whole grain bread made into a garlic-grilled cheese sandwiches. Our mouths still water every time we think of that establishment. Our friends couldn't have been more persuasive in trying to entice us to move west and live near them.

As we visited surrounding communities, they pointed out various housing options for us, *if* we were offered the job. One such community, in our price range, was beautiful and oddly less expensive than other communities. Confused by the pricing difference, we inquired, "Why is this area less expensive?" To which the short answer was, Mt. Rainier. Though currently an inactive volcano, *if* it were to erupt, this specific community would be covered in 40-50 feet of molten lava and ash. Le Anne and I immediately made eye contact. With our life's track record, we would move there just in time to need a cast-iron sailboat. After we laughed, we told them, "No, we better pass on this option."

Our mini getaway was winding down, and it was our final morning. We were sad to be leaving, as our friends took us to the airport. As he drove, I received a call from an unknown Kentucky phone number. It was from our neighbor down the road. I had never spoken to her before, so I thought it strange she would be calling me.

Without introduction she said, "Ya'll been watchin' the news about the big rains here?"

"No, why? Have we had a lot?" I thought her question was an odd way to begin a conversation.

"Well, yes um. In fact, we had so much rain the embankment in front of your house collapsed."

"What?"

"Yeah, some of it even covered the road at the bottom of your hill, and the county had to plow it. Yer house is hangin' on the edge of the hill, and it looks like it might go over the edge any minute!"

"Can you repeat that?"

She obliged, and added in with her Kentucky mountain drawl, "You ain't gonna be able to get up to yer house 'cuz the mudslide buried your driveway." She concluded the call with, "I just felt you'd wanta' know."

I mumbled a thank you, and she hung up. The stunned look on my face had everyone inquisitive. Not sure how to tell everyone what had just happened, my wife exclaimed, "Well, what is it? What's going on back at the house?" Instinctively, she knew the call had to be about the house. I could barely get the words out, trying to sum up what we would be facing, when we arrived home. I blurted out "I'm not sure we may even have a house, when we get back."

The long flight home was much like my flight from the previous week from Florida. I had the same mixed emotions, except this time my wife was sitting beside me. As we talked about the unknowns we faced, we shared tears of dread between moments of levity. Who would believe this latest chapter in our lives? Would my bosses, or even our kids, trust that this new turn of events was even true?

I recounted an incident that had happened while driving home the previous winter. Jesse and I had caught sight of a bright meteor streaking across the dark sky. I had inadvertently let my inner thoughts slip out, "I sure hope that's heading for our house!" He laughed and thought I was kidding – I wasn't.

Appalachian springtime is notoriously rainy but not to this magnitude. The long drive home from the airport was interminable as we dodged multiple small rockslides littering the narrow and twisting mountain roads. As we gazed out our windows, we witnessed evidence of nature's fury from the previous week. Large stately oak trees that had once stood on the mountains were now at the bottom of ravines, half buried in sludge.

Swollen creeks had spilled over their banks. Once quiet, meandering streams were now muddy, angry rivers. There were damaged homes and debris strewn all along the flooded riverbanks. Mud was everywhere.

The closer, we got to home, the more anxiety we felt. As we parked below our hill and gazed upward to the house, we gasped. Where there had previously been a steep vine-covered slope, we now viewed a cavernous hole. In disbelief, we stared upward. From the road, it appeared as if our house was mere inches away from the edge, but in actuality it was about nine feet. The displaced earth from the torrential rains, now covered our driveway, in at least four feet of mud.

In order to gain access to the house, we had to hold onto saplings and vines and climb on our hands and knees as we made our way up the steep incline. It took great effort to retrieve the few belongs that we would need to stay at a local hotel. We didn't know how long we would have to be there, but we were confident we wouldn't be home anytime soon.

We found living in our small town had both benefits and drawbacks. The hotel where we were staying was one that I had used frequently to give temporary shelter to transients passing through our area. The proprietors knew me well, so acquiring a long-term room had not been a problem. Each day Le Anne and I began with a prayer that we would not get any more rain. I made numerous phone calls trying to secure a bulldozer to clear the mud from our driveway. It was of no use; each operator I spoke with had heard of our ongoing house lawsuit and wanted no part of any court proceedings.

A couple of weeks went by and we were unable to obtain the help we needed. My phone calls seemed an exercise in futility and our prayers seemed to go unanswered, but then an idea came to mind. Why not draw up a no-fault document absolving any bulldozer operator of liability? It would offer them peace of mind, if their digging caused further collapse of our embankment. The idea worked, and a dozer operator from a neighboring holler agreed to take the job. We were overjoyed when several dump trucks parked on the narrow road below our hill. Seven dump truck loads or more later, the mud was gone and the driveway became useable again.

We had spent three and a half weeks living in the hotel and were glad to be returning home. On one of the last days of our stay, a divine intervention occurred. Our neighbor, the same one who had given us the warning call on the way to the airport, worked at the hotel. At breakfast she initiated a conversation by asking, "What are you gonna' to do about your hill?"

"Well, our insurance company won't help us because we didn't purchase flood insurance. Who buys flood insurance when you live halfway up a mountain?"

We sadly laughed together at my remark, and then she brightened, "I might know a way you can get some help." At that, she had our full attention.

"There's been a lot of coal and strip mining 'round these parts. Why not call The Division of Mines (DOM)?"

"Why would I do that?"

"If a strip mine had been at the top of yer' mountain, it might be the reason why the rain washed away your hill."

"Where are these people located?"

"They're in Hurricane, West Virginia." (The locals pronounce it, "Her-ah-kin.")

After breakfast, I hurriedly looked up the number and spoke to a sympathetic person at the DOM. She assured me that they would research my inquiry and get back to me. It was probably a longshot but it was worth a try.

The trouble with our area flooding issues was that the politicians could not agree on whether or not the situation should be declared a "disaster." Like us, there were numerous other families affected by the rains. If FEMA (the Federal Emergency Management Agency) would declare the region to be a disaster area, then aid would be forthcoming. About four weeks later, cooler heads prevailed and FEMA came to investigate.

A gentleman carrying a laptop computer walked up our driveway and knocked on our door. "Do the Baker's live here?"

"Yes, I'm John Baker. May I help you?"

He said that he was from FEMA. In order for us to receive their assistance, he would need to ask me some questions. We were surprised by the amount of information that the government had on us. The agent knew (almost to the day) when we were married, how many children we had, where we had lived, and places we had worked. It was quite unnerving, as we correctly confirmed his many inquiries.

Following the interview he said flatly, "Look, we can't offer you monies to repair your hillside, because your house is still standing. It would've had to be destroyed during the weather event in order for us to do that. All we can do is to give you a grant of $2,100 for temporary housing and incidentals." It wasn't the news we were hoping for, but at least our wallets could be replenished for the cost of our hotel stay. As he departed, he told us that our funding would be delivered soon. True to his word, within a week we received by direct deposit our money. God had provided once again!

We tried to assume some normalcy by getting into the swing of serving our churches but living on the side of a cliff and not knowing if the next rainstorm could make the house collapse was stressful. We were grateful our master bedroom was on the backside of the house in the event a worst-case scenario should occur. I envisioned waking up during a rainstorm and having half the house break off and it then resembling an open dollhouse. I tried to make light of our situation by joking that at least the Schwann's truck driver in the area would get a good workout chasing our house down the hill – with us in it.

Most women in families are the keepers of the family heirlooms and treasures and Le Anne was no exception. She set me to work on securing a safer place for the majority of our belongings. We wanted them to be as far away from this mess as possible and in an area not prone to flooding. If the house collapsed, she wanted to minimize our losses. The solution came by way of church members who came from our farthest district to help us pack up the house. They placed everything in the moving truck except our most necessary items. Our church members kindly delivered our boxes and furniture to a storage unit 84 miles away, near their church. We had no idea how long it would be, before it was deemed safe enough to bring our belongings back home.

Our lives had come full circle. We were learning to become minimalists again. With only a bed, a couch, and a desk for furniture, it was if we had just gotten married. We looked as poor as we did back then. For us, the adage, "cut your losses and run," took on a reverse meaning. While we hoped we could cut our losses, who would have thought that possibly in the next rainstorm, it could be our *house* doing the "running."

We endured that house for the duration of our ministry there, and the blue outhouse for five of them. When my wife needed some personal affirmation, she would say (referring to my former college girlfriends), "Do you think what's-her-name would have stayed married to you if she'd had to endure this house *and* the outhouse?"

"Of course not, honey. You're the best!" This exchange would be played and replayed over the many years we owned the house. Come to think of it, she hasn't stopped playing that mantra.

If the Lord had taught us anything about life, it was to live day-to-day, and not look back. We had waited weeks for the fire insurance adjustor to pay us a visit. When he finally presented us with a check to cover the losses from the burned garage, the amount was sufficient to hire a three-man crew of electricians. They begin the arduous process of rewiring the entire house. As they worked, they discovered miracles of their own. There were multiple junction boxes that unbeknownst to us had overheated and smoldered over the years. One of them remarked, "Why your house didn't catch fire before this, is beyond our understanding. Maybe it was the tight-fitting boxes that kept the sparks from spreading."

We gave God all the credit for His continued watch care of us. We were convinced that if it pertained to our house, God had a fulltime job watching over it.

As For Me and My Out House,

Cleaning up after the garage fire next to the powder shed

View at the base of the mudslide when we arrived home

The full mudslide

New French drains added to channel water off the mountain

Retention cages to hold the rocks that rebuilt the embankment

Looking at our home from above where the garage once stood

The last project of the projects, a new concrete driveway

The hillside fully restored

As For Me and My Out House,

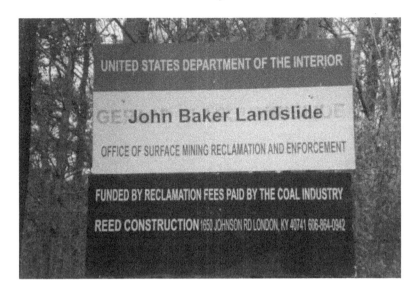

My recognition for being a disaster

The Ultimate Christmas Gift

"And so we celebrated because the Lord had indeed worked miracles for us." Psalm 126:3 (CEV)

Because our house was located on a hillside, it was easy for people to see the lights shining from our windows at night. Living at the end of the county's power line, it was common for our lights to dim or intermittently flash brighter. At times, if viewed from afar, it may have seemed like the rotating beacon of a lighthouse. Happily, our house had just been fully rewired and because of that, we felt much safer during the brownouts and power surges that were all to frequent in our locale. We were relieved that the electrical project was behind us and were now looking forward to the Christmas holiday.

What gift could I give my wife? I knew that celebrities and millionaires planned unique and expensive gifts to give to their spouses and my desire was to do the same. This year I was going to surprise her with a gift that no other woman could boast that she had received. It would be a gift that my wife had wanted for years. It was not jewelry, or anything to wear. As the Twenty Questions guessing game goes, my gift was "bigger than a breadbox."

I had "squirreled away" some of our remaining insurance money, and now I was a man on a mission. I hoped that when my wife found out about my special gift, she would be "flushed" with excitement. I was going to buy her a septic tank!

It had been five long years since the county official had told us that the only acceptable septic tank for our situation would cost in excess of $10,000. Being the owner of a "money-pit" house, the cost might just as well have been a million, but at least with a little over $5,000 to spend I knew I could get something started.

I found a man who promised he could construct a proper septic system for our needs. He would use cement blocks and mortar to build a tank and install a drainage line. No longer would we have to walk outside to use our outhouse. In the winter nights, we would not need to don overcoats on top of our pajamas in order to visit the little shack. The septic contractor who stood before me now, had the contract ready for my signature. I thought … what do I have to lose?

While everyone else had visions of Christmas "sugarplums dancing in their heads", I was intent on getting rid of our Smurf-blue outhouse, with its matching blue-water reservoir. The following week, the man and his small crew surveyed our yard. Despite the fact that our above-ground swimming pool was directly in the middle of the backyard, he was confident they could install the leach lines around it.

Using a bulldozer, they gouged out an eight-foot-deep hole for the tank, and a 100-foot trench for the lines. Soon they began laying cement blocks. From my back porch I watched the bulldozer operator cover the hole with fill dirt and bury the leach line at the far end of the yard. And after two days of work, the system was complete.

As the operator was driving the excavator back toward the porch, he was passing by my treasured swimming pool. For some unknown reason, the backhoe operator's hand slipped and hit the wrong lever. In an instant, the bucket slammed the side wall of the pool and made a big gash in its side. All I could do was watch helplessly as 13,000 gallons of water gushed out into the yard and flowed down the embankment. Our ruined and useless pool resembled a grounded ship with a hole in its hull. The attached wood decking was now as useful as dental floss at a nursing home concert.

By way of an apology, the operator simply shrugged his shoulders. "Well," He said, "It was in the way. I tried to avoid it!" I remember thinking … "I am glad that this man isn't a brain surgeon". The project now complete, I just wanted this crew gone. I hoped we would never see them again. Dealing with faulty and ill-trained contractors is the sure-fire way to become cranky. Taking note that the pool was a total loss, he offered to drag the liner and the aluminum sides to our burned-out garage area. His parting words were, "Maybe you can bury it later."

My only consolation, as he drove away, was the realization that our outhouse would be history in a few days. Each day when I left the house, I couldn't help but see the heap of ripped pool liner, and the collapsed aluminum sides. They gave me the impression that a hurricane had passed through our yard. Despite the voluminous blue mess, it was still an encouraging sign of hope. It reminded me that fragments of optimism could still be found amidst chaos.

By the end of the week, five years to the day after it had arrived, our outhouse was taken down our driveway on a journey to its new location. In the years we had rented it, we had become friends with the company's driver. On the days he had come to clean and service it, he had brought treats for our dog Goldie. In exchange for his kindness, we had often given him homemade bread, books, or vegetables from our garden. During his many visits, we had talked about what it meant to be a Christian, family issues, and current events. As we said our final goodbyes, we knew we would probably never see him again.

As we watched the little blue shack leave our property, we stood amazed that even this simple outhouse had been used in the service of the Lord. I wonder if God smiled at the irony of an outhouse having a fitting ending.

The Designated Honor

"But if I were you, I would appeal to God; I would lay my cause before him. He performs wonders that cannot be fathomed, miracles that cannot be counted. He provides rain for the earth; he sends water on the countryside." Job 5:8-10 (NIV)

The phone rang in our kitchen, so I grabbed it.

"Is this Mr. John Baker?"

"Yes, it is may I help you?"

"I'm calling from the Division of Mines." The man's voice was kind, and calmly matter of fact. "I'm one of the engineers who has been investigating the reason for your hillside collapse."

My heart began to beat faster as I listened.

"But we've been stumped by something on your property."

"Oh? What might that be?"

"You have a cement structure near the top of your driveway."

"You mean our root cellar?"

"Well, actually it isn't." The man paused. "We believe it's a powder shed. It has the same build and dimensions as one. That's what is confusing us."

"What's a powder shed?"

"It's a building made to securely house charges and dynamite used in mining operations. The powder shed suggests that somewhere on your property there had to have been a coal mining operation. In order to confirm that, it needs to be authenticated by a topological or structure contour map. We've been trying to find one."

I began to see a glimmer of hope that our massive problem might be resolved. He explained that engineers from a neighboring state had visited our property three times. Each time they had seen the shed but were unable to connect or confirm whether a mining operation had existed. Without a legal map, or a mining survey showing the history, our restoration project could not be granted approval. The engineer assured me that they were still searching the map archives. As our conversation ended, I felt disappointed, but hopeful. Maybe he could help us, so we continued to pray.

It was almost three weeks to the day when the engineer called again. He promised this time he would personally visit our property. What he didn't say was that he had some very big news. He arrived on a beautiful clear summer day and parked his truck in our driveway. I could see that he was a man in his fifties. His voice was soft-spoken and friendly. He got straight to work assessing our property. I waited on our back porch as he climbed with his clipboard the steep hill behind our house. I knew he was trying to confirm signs of a prior mining operation. I thought … at least the weather was not unbearably hot for him. Though there were some stray clouds, the forecast called for warm temperatures with a slight chance of showers.

As he neared the crest of our expansive hill, God had other plans for the weather at that moment. Without warning, there was a stabbing flash of lightening followed by an instant thunderclap. Where had that come from? Minutes before, the sun was shining, and the sky was blue. By the time the engineer had made a hasty retreat to our back door, the heavens had opened up and he became thoroughly drenched by the unexpected deluge.

While we stood under the eaves of the house watching mother nature's wrath, he began by asking me how we had obtained the property. He listened intently as I shared our seven-and-a-half-year odyssey for justice. He told of his own challenges involving the recent loss of his wife, and how he too had found strength from his faith. God's faithfulness became the topic intwined in our conversation. Despite our many setbacks, we agreed that God had been the anchor in both our lives. A prayer for courage on both our parts was injected in the conversation.

As we watched the ensuing torrent of runoff gush toward the bottom of the rocky hillside, it restarted a little waterfall near our shed. Within a short time, deep ruts were forming in the driveway all the way to a culvert below. We stood silently watching the unrelenting overflow course its way across the property.

Only after the rain had begun to let up, the man slowly turned and stated, "Mr. Baker, you have a problem that *was* caused by a former strip mine operation. I know this because a few days ago we discovered an obscure map dated from 1962. It proves that there was a strip mine here on your mountain. Today, I witnessed the rapid runoff firsthand. Your hillside was never properly channeled." With calm assurance he continued, "The Division of Mines is going to make this right. The federal government will pay for restoring your property to its original intent."

Just like that, God had answered our prayers in a monumental way! For a moment it seemed too good to be true. I was glad my face was already wet from rain, or the engineer would have seen the tears of joy trickling down my cheeks. Le Anne and I had always felt that before we could ever take on a new church assignment, our house problems would have to be resolved first. God gave us that answer, as only He could!

Before the man departed, he explained what the next steps would be. In about a month, contracting crews from around the state would assemble in our yard on a designated day and submit bids for the cost of restoring the property. He informed me that the payment for the project would be borne by a federal excise tax collected on coal. For every ton of coal produced, the government levies a small tax on coal operators. The money is then kept in escrow so that even if a coal company goes out of business, their errors can still be resolved.

The following month, as promised, our driveway began to fill up with pickup trucks. The mining representative used our front porch to conduct business like an auctioneer. There were numerous questions that needed to be answered before the bidding process could begin. One question made us laugh out loud, but we were certain no one would understand the reason for our levity. A contractor shouted, "This job is going to take some time. Does anyone know of a company that can deliver a portable outhouse to the site?"

I felt like a third grader who stands up in class and loudly shouts, "I know, I know, pick me!" I smiled a little as I assured the gathered crews that I could most definitely provide them with a phone number.

The bidding process was over almost as quickly as it had begun. The winning proposal came in at $84,000. This matched the exact amount we had been defrauded on our home;

excluding the property. I told the contractor that we would be happy to hand him the keys to everything, if we could walk away with that amount. He smiled but said it didn't work that way. Our property needed a vast French drain, a runoff drainage line, a shored-up embankment, and most likely a new concrete driveway. A few weeks later, the little blue building, we always jokingly referred to as our "second mortgage", made a return engagement to our back yard. It had come back home, if only for a little while!

In my life, I have seen impressive honors bestowed upon many great individuals. Buildings, bridges, and parks have all been given the names of distinguished persons. Yet, to my dismay no grand honor ever awaited me—until now. Instead of a grand honor, I was given the distinction of having a natural disaster named after me. Emblazoned at the top of our driveway, where any passersby could see, a large wooden sign proclaimed, **The John Baker Mudslide**. How fitting that I was named after a disaster! I'm confident my mother would have concurred. To this day, whenever I am tempted to become a little inflated in ego, I pull out the picture of the disaster sign and it serves to remind me to remain humble and maintain a good sense of humor.

It was difficult to stay out of the way of the of heavy equipment since the crew operated from sunrise to sunset. Standing on our front porch was the best seat in the house, the heavy equipment mere feet from our front door. Dozens of trucks were either hauling fill away trees and fill or were bringing in rocks of various dimensions. For the first time in the crew's land restoration projects, they were using a new form of hill retention. They were forming chicken wire cages and filling them with heavy boulders. Laid in tiers, one on top of the other, the missing embankment would be recreated and reinforced with those descending and layered boxes. Over the weeks it took to complete, it was a common sight to see our narrow road lined with waiting dump trucks. There was so much construction traffic, that a workman had to be posted in front of the blind curve at the bottom of our driveway out on the road.

The avalanche of dirt being moved to accommodate the new wire cages was also the precursor to a cavalcade of encouraging news. The federal government wanted to finally settle our lawsuit. In just a few short months, the Lord had been working on our behalf, with lightning speed.

Following seven years of countless court proceedings and depositions, our trial was paused in favor of forcing us into federal mediation instead. At the onset of negotiations the price they offered us was laughable. The government attorney told us in the afternoon, "agree with the settlement amount, or risk having your case drag on into infinity." He added for good measure, if you decline our offer, you may get nothing by the time the trial occurs, if there is any trial." With the possibility of receiving nothing at the end, we still dug in our heels and told the parties we absolutely had to have $4000 more than they offered, or we'd walk. Seeing our resolve, they acquiesced, and the all-day proceedings ended with an agreed settlement of .66 cents on the dollar. Having fought the good fight for so long, we were relieved the fight was finally over.

As we left the courthouse, the house's previous owner descended the granite staircase from a distance behind us. He was irate and apparently wanted to get something off of his chest, now that the trial was over. My wife and daughter became nervous as he yelled at us from across the street. Visibly angry, he asserted we had lied, and that the damages we claimed were fraudulent because his workmanship was "stellar." I let him rant; a response would be useless. Sometimes the best way to deal with confrontation is to walk away and keep your peace. I slowly turned and made my way to our car. His words no longer mattered to us. Despite being shorted on compensation, the evidence of fraud had been proven conclusively. For nine years we had endured a most difficult life because of his deceit and lies; I refused to spend one more minute going forward on his lack of integrity.

Finally, the three-week land restoration and embankment project was completed. My bosses rejoiced with us by sending a skilled work crew called Helping Hands to begin the final repairs on the infrastructure of the house. We agreed to pay all the crew's food and lodging and to buy the needed supplies for the project. The hardworking men jacked up the back of the house, replaced broken and disintegrating floor joists, and laid down new hardwood flooring. Where there had once been rotted wood and sloping door frames, new French doors were added. Each day the crew worked, my wife made heaps of food for them to enjoy. I was the "gopher" that made all the trips to town for materials. Within a few weeks, their full-time task had been completed. Each crewmember received a thank you card and gift from us, before they departed.

After a prayer of thanksgiving and mercies for safe travels home, they all made their way down our driveway and drove off. We looked around the property in awe. With the combined talents of all the crews, and the grace of God, our property had been transformed to look like new. The burned-down garage foundation had been bulldozed away and replaced with a gently sloping green lawn. Large gravel-covered French drains redirected the rainwater from the mountain into controlled channels that no longer washed out the driveway. The part gravel and part cracked cement driveway had been replaced with a long, and full sleek concrete version. Our embankment was now tiered and secured by unmovable cages of stone. Our plumbing and electrical problems were over. The downed trees from the project offered us new sweeping views of the farmland below us. The house was, for the first time, up to code. The finished project had taken nine long years to complete!

Confident that the restoration of our home was the sign, God would give us to move on, we were at peace that our life in Appalachia was coming to an end. We were confident that now that our prayers had been answered, we would be rewarded with a healthy profit from the sale of our house. The anticipated profit would be used to purchase another home, wherever God would send us next. It was time to put it up our home for sale.

The first couple who viewed our home agreed to pay the full asking price. We were giddy thinking our financial woes would soon be behind us. This sale would lift the fog of our financial hardships, we would be paid back for the misery of our home's nightmare. But our optimism was fleeting. Sadly, the couple's financing fell through. Never again did an interested buyer look at our property!

One of God's overlooked kindnesses to us is that He doesn't reveal our earthly future. I'm sure it would break our hearts if we knew sometimes. We did heed His call by accepting a new position in Tennessee. The beautifully restored home we left behind (regardless of all of our efforts) was lost to foreclosure two years later. We had borrowed all that was allowed from my retirement fund, hoping the house would sell within two years, but sadly it wasn't to be. The house's past history was apparently too-widely known in our small community to interest any buyer. Our net loss on the house topped $46,000.

I jokingly called the loss of our house, "divorce-light" – while I lost the house, I did keep my wife. Despite losing it, I truly did get the better part of the deal.

To this day, our former home on that beautiful mountainside has sat empty for over a decade. On moving day, as we walked through the empty house for the final time, I did what I had done countless times before while exiting – I switched off the light. That simple action was a reminder that God requires us to do something similar in our own lives. Remember the tears and laughter, but when He requires us to move in a new direction, don't forget to shut off the light to your past. Each day begins a new journey. Keep your eyes on Jesus, and trust His plan, no matter the outcome. We find solace that God's Word promises that we are going to get everything we have ever lost back and then some in the end. The only requirement in receiving it, is to remain faithful in our relationship with God. What a promise that is!

"He's Gonna Drown Grandma!"

"Let us hold unswervingly to the hope we profess, for he who promised is faithful."
Hebrews 10:23 (NIV)

In the book, *"Even the Angels Must Laugh Sometimes,"* by Jan S. Doward (1984), the author writes about many real-life funny experiences from various churches. Someday, I believe one of my own adventures may end up in a sequel to his book.

It was my final weekend as pastor in our Appalachian churches, so it only seemed fitting that we conclude our ministerial assignment by having a baptism. The candidate was a lovely older woman who had been consigned to a wheelchair due to her declining health. It was her desire to "take the plunge" for God, and it seemed an appropriate choice in the sweltering month of July. For logistical reasons, it was impossible for her to be baptized at church. The church's baptismal tank was not handicap accessible, and the lady was, well… pleasantly girthy. It was decided that an outdoor service would alleviate both issues.

The soon-to-be interim pastor accompanied me to a local lake on the day before we were to have the service. We assumed that we would need a gently sloping boat ramp for an access point to the lake. We found one, and as if sent by God, a fisherman in a small boat was floating about 25 yards away from where we were standing. Calling out to him, we asked if he had a depth-finder. He hollered back that he did. When we asked him how deep the water was, he called back that at the lower end of the ramp it was 8 feet. He cautioned that beyond the ramp, the lake had an abrupt drop off of 20 feet or more. Satisfied we had found a good spot for the baptismal service, we reported back to the church family that we were set for the weekend.

The day of the service was hot and overcast. Soon all the church members and the candidate in her wheelchair arrived. While the lady was being courteously pushed toward the ramp, the members sauntered down to the water's edge to watch the ceremony. The guest evangelist and a church deacon were patiently standing in the green-tinged water. They were making sure there were no rocks on the ramp that might cause a mishap. The plan was to take the candidate halfway down the ramp until she was waist deep in water, help her to stand, and then perform the baptism.

I waited for her at the side of the ramp, so I could personally guide her wheelchair into the water. Concerned that she might tip out of the chair as we followed the downward angle of the ramp, I turned her around. In my bare feet, I rolled the wheelchair carefully backward down the ramp toward the lake. Mentally, I went over my checklist: baptismal robe ... check ... swim trunks ... check ... towel ... check ... slope and angle ... already checked ... access point ... good.

The one thing I was not prepared for was that the boat ramp would be slick with green algae. I felt the grooves of the long ramp underneath my feet, and carefully positioned her wheelchair for a gradual descent. As my feet and ankles eased deeper into the murky water, a sudden change of plan occurred. We found ourselves hurtling down toward the lake, and gathering speed. My size 12 ½ feet could not contend with the algae-covered metal ramp. I was helpless to slow our rapid descent toward a hazardous deep-water dunking. The woman, realizing that our situation was out of control, began flailing her arms and legs. The result of her thrashing movements *increased* our momentum.

Out of the corner of my eye, I could see the bewildered looks on the faces of the crowd along the shore. Why was their pastor running backward with the lady in the wheelchair? Didn't he know what was about to happen? The evangelist and his assistant could do nothing to stop us; we slid past them like "a jet ski taking off at full throttle".

The moment was captioned by the woman's young grandson. On the shore, he was frantically waving his bottle of Mountain Dew, like a warning flag. He screamed repeatedly, "He's gonna drown grandma! He's gonna drown grandma!"

In that split second, I thought he was probably right, and I mentally prepared for our fate of slipping into the depths beyond the end of the ramp. At the last possible moment, in what can only be described as a miracle, the runaway wheelchair and I stopped motionless on the ramp, as if we had come up against an invisible wall. We were only a foot away from sinking into oblivion. The water was now lapping at the chin of my panicky candidate.

With the help of the deacon and evangelist we were able to pull her wheelchair partially back up the ramp, help the lady stand, and ready her to be dipped. The actual act of baptizing her was the easy part. Getting her all the way back up the ramp was now the challenge.

With every ounce of energy I could muster, I gripped the underwater grooves of the ramp with my toes, and slowly pushed her wheelchair back up the slope. As she began to emerge from the lake water, the church members sang the familiar song, "Shall We Gather at the River," by Robert Lowry (1864). I later whispered to the choir director, "You were singing the wrong song. You should have been singing: "We Have an Anchor," by Priscilla J. Owens, (1882).

It was fitting, that on my last weekend at my little church, I would experience both a high and a low situation. It was the "swan song" of our ministerial time there. That special day gave us one additional reason to be thankful. We were glad that the scene on the ramp had not been preserved forever on YouTube!

The event offered me a new perspective. I had almost presided over my first ever drive-in baptism. I imagined calling my bosses to tell them … I have good news and bad news. We added a new church member today, but I had to cross her name off the books because I accidently drowned her.

Living nine years in Appalachia, our family had learned many valuable life lessons. Our stories didn't always end the way we wanted, but that didn't mean the "book" was finished. God may not have called us just to be successful at bringing in new members. He called us to be faithful also. We know the seeds of goodwill that we planted will bear fruit for many years to come. We had been set on a difficult path, but we took solace knowing that we could still give praise for the challenges along the way.

During our arduous Kentucky years, we developed a solid, unwavering relationship with Jesus. At the end, in spite of all our adversities, we found that our humor was still intact. It was the place that God had brought us to, and it had become a chapter of faith and miracles.

We now look for hidden blessings in all things. Our new home, in our current ministerial assignment, features three bathrooms. The best part is–they are all *inside* the house.

> "And so we celebrated
> because the Lord had indeed
> worked miracles for us." Psalm 126:3 (CEV)

Epilogue

by Le Anne Baker with Connie Mallon
What to do while you're waiting on God

1. **Pray, pray, pray-** This is going to be your lifeline. Talking to God keeps the lines of communication open so you can be attuned to His leading. He is always listening and cares about you and your personal problems. He has promised to be with us no matter what the situation. Remember: if you are praying about your problem, then God is already working on it. See Philippians 4:6-7, 1Peter 5:7, Joshua 1:9, Psalm 16:8

2. **Cling to God's promises –**. Do whatever is necessary to keep God's words in your mind: pray from the scriptures, speak them out loud, sing them, repeat them all day long, memorize them, write them out, tape them to your refrigerator and bathroom mirror, or even to your car's steering wheel. Keep them ever before you and believe them. Remember, these are God's word's speaking directly to *your* problem. See Isaiah 41:10, 12:2.

3. **No complaining** – The children of Israel wandered around in the desert for 40 years to make what would have ordinarily been an 11-day trip. What kept them in the wilderness was their lack of trust in God's power, and their constant grumbling. Complaining prolongs difficulties and won't solve problems. God is looking for people who will speak positively over their situation, "calling things that are not as though they are" Romans 4:17, paraphrased. The positive attitude tells others, and Satan, that you are trusting God, and not man, for your answers. (See also Exodus 15:2). View your problem as a way to trust Him more. If you are finding it hard to stay optimistic, find some Christian books on your subject. There are many authors who can share their experiences and godly wisdom, while offering the reader great encouragement and much-needed hope.

4. **Do *your* part so God can do *His*-**You both have a part to play. If you need a job but have never sent out a resume, how can a potential employer know you are out there? If you are having financial trouble but have never made a budget, how can you expect God to help you pay your bills? Put your faith into action and allow God to work on your behalf. Trust Him and watch His mighty hand at work.

5. **Evaluate your past choices.** Has God given you a task you didn't complete? Did He ask you to give something away that you are still keeping? Did He give you a directive that you haven't followed? You cannot expect a blessing on your current situation if you have not obeyed His requests in the past. Ask Him to show

you what needs to change, confess it, ask for forgiveness, correct it, and move on.

6. **Invest time in someone else who is hurting.** This is a very important spiritual principle that my husband and I learned along the way. What you make happen for others, God will make happen for you; this is the "Golden Rule" in action. You are making deposits into God's "bank" so when the time comes, you will be able to make that all-important withdrawal in your time of need. By getting your mind off of yourself and on to helping others, it will open the door for God to work on behalf of your situation. Matthew 7:12.

7. **Avoid "what if" scenarios** – Worrying about what might happen, will only increase your level of fear and uncertainty. When we approach a situation with "if we do this then they will do that," then we are not trusting God to solve our problem. "What if" thinking allows Satan to use fear against us, steal our joy, and leave us spiritually powerless. Fear is the number one tool he uses to paralyze us and keep us from making progress. The Old Testament prophet, Nehemiah, reminds us in verse 8:10 where our focus should be; that the joy of the Lord is our strength.

8. **Maintain a normal routine as much as possible-** This is critical, especially if children are involved. It helps to maintain some semblance of order, because as humans we thrive on routine. It not only gives a sense of normalcy in an unstable situation but helps us mentally, if we can be in control of some part of our life. A routine

can keep us from feeling helpless, when life spins out of control. This is not saying that we are not to trust God any less. We can still let Him be in charge of the situation. He gives us a brain and expects us to be rational and smart while trusting Him at the same time. See 2 Timothy 1:7.

9. **Take care of your health–**Eat a well-balanced diet, take your vitamins, exercise, stay hydrated, and if possible, get an adequate amount of sleep. You will be able to think more clearly and make more rational decisions. Believe it or not, this is spiritual warfare. When we are tired and worn out, we become vulnerable to Satan's attacks, allowing him to come at us with a vengeance. He is looking for any open door or tiny crack in our lives to gain a foothold. And if he does get a foothold, he is liable to establish a stronghold.

10. **Keep your sense of humor-** Humor is God's gift to keep us mentally and physically healthy. Laughing is like internal jogging. Remember- A merry heart is as good as medicine! Proverbs 17:22 (paraphrased). Making light of your situation does not mean you are denying what is going on, but it keeps you from getting overly stressed and worried about the things you cannot control. Seek out friends with a keen sense of humor to help you stay focused on what is important. This will keep you from wallowing in your problem and allows for a much-needed outlet. It's also important to do something fun. Take the kids to the zoo, go for a bike ride, have a picnic. This will keep your mind off

of your issues, temporarily put your situation on "pause" and renew your energy to face another day.

What *not* to say to someone who is going through difficulties

1. **Use common sense and sensitivity**-Now is not the time to discuss your new house remodel or your upcoming anniversary cruise. They need words of comfort and a listening ear. Discussing what you are doing will only create more pain for them and be perceived as uncaring or callous. When one of our friends was going through cancer treatments, an insensitive person remarked "Since you're not going to make it anyway, could you say hi to my mom and dad for me when you get to Heaven?" Please, think before you speak.

2. **"I know exactly how you feel".** Chances are, you probably don't. Your situation may have been similar, but no two people have the exact same problem and circumstances. No one can know exactly how you feel except Jesus. Instead, try saying something like "I can tell this is really hurting you. Would you like to talk about it?"

3. **"I know what I'd do if I was in your situation".** If you can't solve all your own problems, don't try to solve someone else's. Offering unsolicited advice is both rude and selfish, leaving the impression that you are smarter and far more knowledgeable. The last thing they need is to have someone make them feel foolish, insignificant, or more confused. What they need is someone to

listen to them in a nonjudgmental way. Try responding with a statement like this: I don't understand why this is happening, but I am here for you if you need someone to lean on.

4. **"You have such bad luck"**. Luck has nothing to do with it. Whatever is happening has been filtered through God's hand first. He knows the end from the beginning and has the person's best interest at heart.

5. **"With all the trouble you've had, you must be doing something wrong"**- Someone actually said this to us! Making this statement implies the person's relationship to God is in question. They might not be doing anything wrong. God may be using this as a test of faith, a building process or even a witness to someone else who is watching. You never know. Don't give your assessment for God's judgement.

6. **"God must be trying to teach you something"**- The person going through all these difficulties has already considered this possibility. Don't contribute to their anxiety and cast doubt on their relationship with God. Instead, encourage them with uplifting words of faith and hope. Pray with them. Send them encouraging scriptures to help them through their darkest days. Let them know you are lifting them up in prayer. Take them to lunch; do whatever it takes to let them know you care and that they are not forgotten. After all, God might be trying to teach *you* something.

7. **"God won't give you more than you can bear"** - To the person with the difficulties, this is not encouraging. While this statement may be true, reiterating it will be perceived as being careless and unhelpful. They may barely be able to get through the day as it is and feel as though they are ready to go under. The thought of having to deal with tomorrow is just one more added stress point. Mother Theresa understood this scripture all too well, but she often added, "I just wish He (God) wouldn't trust me so much."

8. **"I've had some of your luck before"** - Again, luck has nothing to do with it; life happens to everyone. Matthew 5:45 says it rains on the just and unjust meaning that blowing a tire on the way to an important meeting can happen to a Christian just as easily as an atheist. This only draws further attention to their difficulties and makes them feel worse. Christians are to be in the business of restoration and encouragement so avoid this kind of statement.

About the Author

John and Le Anne Baker have been married thirty-seven years and have served in the pastoral ministry for more than twenty years in New Hampshire, Kentucky, and Tennessee. They are both seminar presenters having trained audiences in marriage reconciliation, conflict coaching, how to promote yourself in a tough job market, and praying for your partner. John's career path has included stints in radio broadcasting, long-term care administration, foodservice, public relations, hospital chaplaincy, and he was twice elected president of the Kentucky Dietary Managers Association. He is a graduate of Johnson State College in Vermont. His wife Le Anne is a graduate of Murray State University in Kentucky.

Printed in the USA
CPSIA information can be obtained
at www.ICGtesting.com
LVHW091305250124
769289LV00003B/433